What are you
waiting for?

At the age of 25 Justin was sick of falling short of his goals, so he decided to take control of his life and use his last $50 to start his own business. With no experience behind him, he had to learn quickly to survive and, eventually, to thrive in the business world. Several years on—and a lot of hard work and determination later—Attitude Inc.® is now a multimillion-dollar company, and Justin has retired from the everyday running of the business. Justin now speaks full time, motivating and inspiring audiences around the world, and is currently developing his latest business venture, Attitude Performance Coaching. So much for retirement!

What are you
waiting for?

justin herald

IF NOTHING CHANGES,
NOTHING CHANGES

ALLEN&UNWIN

First published in 2004

Allen & Unwin
83 Alexander Street
Crows Nest NSW 2065
Australia
Phone: (61 2) 8425 0100
Fax: (61 2) 9906 2218
Email: info@allenandunwin.com
Web: www.allenandunwin.com

National Library of Australia
Cataloguing-in-Publication entry:

Herald, Justin.
    What are you waiting for?: if nothing changes, nothing changes.

    ISBN 1 74114 186 9.

    1. Self-actualisation (Psychology). 2. Success.
    3. Motivation (Psychology). I. Title.

158.1

Text design by Tabitha King
Set in 10/14 pt Sabon by Midland Typesetters, Maryborough, Victoria
Printed in Australia by McPherson's Printing Group

10 9 8 7 6 5 4 3

This book is dedicated to
all those people whose
goal or dream is yet to
become a reality.

BE A BETTER YOU!

Contents

Introduction

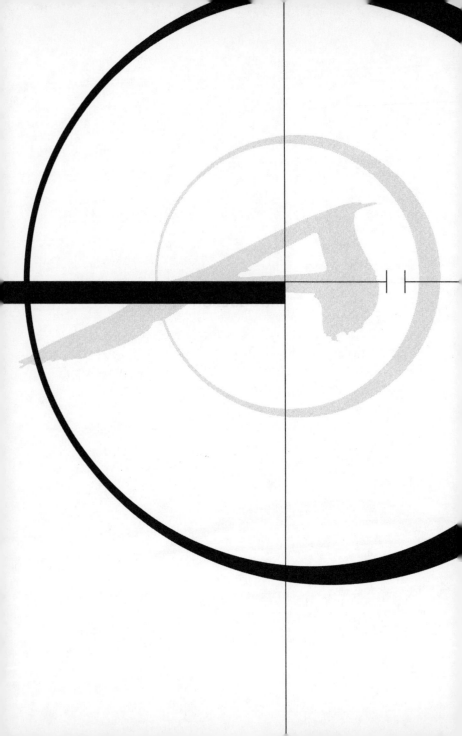

Well, who would have thought it, a second book?

If you had asked any of my teachers at school if they thought that I'd ever be an author, and a bestselling author (so they say), I can guarantee that the reply would have been mixed with the sounds of roaring laughter. It just goes to show that no matter where you have come from, what you have done or what others think you will achieve, anything and everything is possible.

This book has been written as a result of my understanding of where I have come from and where I am going, and of the challenges I have overcome along the way. It is intended for all those people who want to achieve something for themselves, for all who have goals and dreams that one day they would like to fulfil. Whether it is a big goal or a small goal doesn't really matter.

What are you waiting for? is about the journey to success, and the issues and problems I believe need to be understood and overcome along the way. What I am talking about is the principle of change—that is, the changes we need to make in our lives before we start our journey and the changes we need to address once we reach some level of success. Some of the issues you are about to read about will reoccur constantly, even when you reach a level of success.

This book is not meant to make you feel bad or to highlight your negative points. It has been written as a guide to help you along your journey towards those goals and dreams—which for some of you may have been set many years ago and remain a source of frustration. For those of you who have reached some of your goals, this book is meant to serve as a reminder that you should never let yourself stop addressing the area of change.

I am occasionally irritated by media interviews where the reporter comes out with the tired old line, 'Justin Herald—the overnight success'. It took me many years to become an overnight success! Nothing happened to me overnight. I didn't just wake up one morning and BANG, find success staring me in the face, and I can guarantee that success will not come to you that way either.

The whole 'get rich quick and become an overnight success' phenomenon has gone too far and puts way too much unrealistic pressure on people. There is no such thing as overnight success—it's a myth. There is no secret to success; there is no special formula that you can apply to make sure that everything you touch will work. Anyone who believes that is just kidding themselves.

Today, more than ever, there is a trend to find the quick fix that will give you all of your dreams and goals in one fell swoop, without making any changes and without even raising a sweat. But you won't make it overnight, nor should you think that it is possible. Many have tried and many have failed. Success just isn't that simple or easy—if it was then everyone would be successful. That being the fact, it is up to you, and only you, to get off your backside and back on track towards those things you are yet to accomplish. Being successful and reaching our own levels of success is not so much about the finish line, it is more about what we need to address along the way so that success is longer lasting.

Success takes many years of forming, moulding and understanding. Yes, I know what you are thinking already. You may know some people who became successful very quickly. But *how* quickly was it? Do you know how long they were working at achieving those goals and dreams that they have mastered? I challenge you to look at the time and effort it took them to get there in the end. Or if success did happen to them 'overnight', or very quickly, I wonder if they will be able to sustain that success for a long period of time? You see, for most of us, all we see in other people—successful people—is the end result. What we don't see are the hurdles and heartaches they faced along the way.

In this book I talk about the continuing changes that I had to address and understand during the course of my own success over the years. I believe that the changes that worked for me, if applied and woven into your journey and your thinking, will enable you to move closer to those goals you have set for yourself. There may be some areas that you will see as plain common sense. But you would be surprised how uncommon common sense is these days.

There is no blanket quick-fix method that can be applied to everyone and every situation. Each of us has different areas that need to be addressed. If you think for one minute that you can remain who you are today for the rest of your life and still achieve everything you desire, you are in for a big shock and a whole lot of frustration and disappointment.

There are a lot of people looking like they are doing things to better themselves and their situations. They are making all the right movements, but in reality all they are doing is treading water. Sure they are staying afloat, but they aren't moving in a forward direction. Even if your progress isn't as quick as you had originally planned, you have to keep moving forward.

Please don't think that you are going to end up a broken mess by the time you finish reading this book. It should be the exact opposite. I want you to excel in every area of your life— both personal and work—but the only way that will happen is if you address the areas that are keeping you bogged down. Some of you may even think that none of the following is aimed at you, but I challenge you to look deep and hard at where you are at in your life and the areas that you know are holding you back. Face the changes that need to be made, then move on. Don't waste your time dwelling on the negative; be positive about where you want to go in your life. Apply what you read in this book to your situation right now.

Remember though, there is no prize for finishing first when it comes to your personal goals and dreams. Stickability is the key: make sure that your goals and dreams will be with you for years to come. That will happen if the foundation of who you are is built on sound, solid and ethical principles.

I remember my father telling a story of Sir Winston Churchill visiting an exclusive boys' school. His arrival was much anticipated; everyone was eager to hear him speak. As Churchill rose to the platform and walked over to the lectern there was a hushed silence. You could have heard a pin drop. Everyone was on the edge of their seat waiting to hear words of wisdom from this great leader.

After what seemed like hours, he said only three words—but they changed the course of the lives of many who heard them. He said: 'NEVER GIVE UP.' That was all, and then he sat down.

That is my advice to you as well. Never, never, never give up. It is just too easy. Some of you may have built walls around yourself as an excuse to justify why you have yet to achieve all that you want. Push through those barriers that have been blocking your path. Keep focused on what you want to achieve in your life.

Success isn't just a word with seven letters in it, it is a lifestyle choice. If I hadn't changed, nothing would have changed. But first I had to recognise the various areas I needed to change. Be different . . . be better. So, what are you waiting for?

The principle of
positive thinking

1

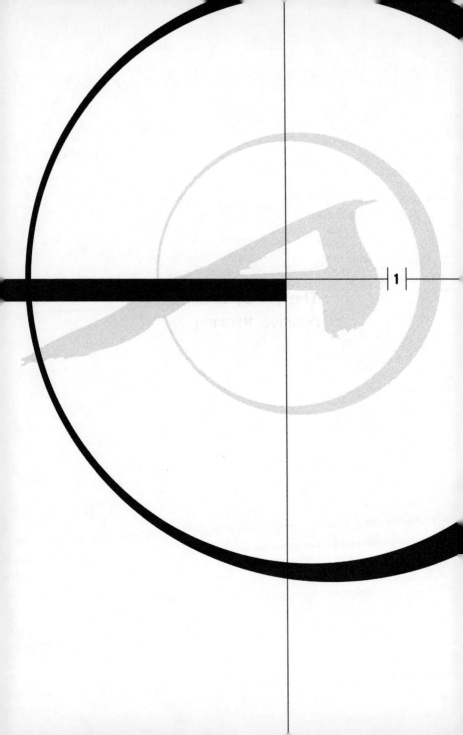

In today's environment of 'rah rah' speakers and 'rah rah' books, we are constantly being told to 'think positive'—but what does that actually mean? It is all too easy to miss the importance of thinking positively, of positive influences and positive environments. Too often we are quick to dismiss this particular key to success because of the hype that surrounds the whole positive-thinking area.

When I was growing up, the picture I had in my head of someone who was always positive, was of a guy in a safari suit with thick black-rimmed glasses and no personality, ranting and raving about the benefits of having a positive outlook.

In reality, without the influence of a positive environment and a positive mentality, we will always continue to struggle to get what we want out of life. Just as I am a black or white type of thinker, I have to say that I put most experiences into two categories as well: positive or negative. You see, when you keep your thinking simple and positive, your actions will be easier to administer because you don't have all of the clutter getting in the way.

When you start looking at every opportunity and setting your goals from a perspective of positivity, not negativity, you will find those opportunities or goals easier to reach. When negative thinking gets in the way, all that does, basically, is put into your thinking, then in turn into your actions, all the reasons you think you can't achieve them. You have basically talked yourself out of wanting to achieve what you desire before you have even started. For some, the negative outlook on life is a lot easier to handle than a positive one. When you're negative, you don't need to address change. You can just stay the same miserable you forever. No wonder so many people are still chasing their dreams and goals—they haven't replaced their negative thinking with positive thinking. It is only when we start operating from a positive point that we can challenge our thinking and actions.

'So,' I can already hear half of you saying to yourselves, 'how do I change my thinking?' If it was really easy then everyone would be positive and have a positive approach to life. What is simple, though, are some of the steps that can get you to turn around your thinking, from a negative and somewhat defeated approach to one that is willing to give anything a try regardless of the perceived possibility of failure. Giving up is just too easy. Stopping before any results have time to show themselves is all too common.

When I was little I remember reading a book called *The Little Red Caboose*. It was about a little train that was fully loaded, making its way up a very steep mountain. Halfway up the mountain it started to run out of steam. The little train then started saying to itself, 'I think I can, I think I can, I think I can'—and the result was that it talked itself up and over that mountain.

The point of telling you that children's story is to demonstrate the principle of a positive mind as well as positive words. You will face difficult times throughout your journey through life and your journey towards success, and you will make mistakes. If you allow yourself and your thinking to be tainted by those setbacks, then you only have yourself to blame for slowing down your progress.

Now I am not saying that you have to talk to yourself every day to get ahead, but what I am pointing out is the importance of surrounding yourself with as many positive influences as you can, your thinking and your words being on top of that list.

The first step is to surround yourself with positive-thinking people. Now I don't mean those types of people who make out that it never rains for them and life is just wonderful. You know the ones who you would swear had just come out of a 1940s romance movie? They just aren't real or even relevant. What I mean is you need to have people around you who see the bigger picture in their own lives and in turn can see and understand what you are trying to achieve.

I don't want people around me who constantly tell me that what I am trying to achieve is impossible. I want people who will challenge me to think bigger and higher than I had previously thought. I don't mean that I only want 'yes men' around me either. You know the ones who always agree with everything you are doing because they're scared that if they disagree you won't speak to them again?

Many of us are very selective about what brand of food we buy, what type of shampoo we put in our hair (not me), even what type of food we buy our dogs, but we seem to let just anyone influence our goals and dreams by letting their negative words affect our journey.

We all seem to think that our friends will always have our best interests at heart. Well, let me give it to you straight: IT DOESN'T WORK LIKE THAT!!! I am going to give you an example. (I will probably get in trouble from my wife later, but it will be too late by then as the book will already be finished and printed. Phew.)

Vanessa is always meeting new people. As Vanessa has a very infectious personality she is constantly growing her circle of friends; people are drawn to her and all that she has to give. What I have noticed is that some of these new friends don't have the same positive outlook that Vanessa and her best friends have. I see it starting to affect her sometimes. I believe these women are drawn to Vanessa and her existing friends because of their positive outlook on life, but the problem is that once some of them are settled into the circle of friendship they revert back to their old selves. By that, I mean negative, controlling and sometimes downright rude.

This not only annoys me, but it also gets to Vanessa and her other friends as their environment begins to change from one that is very positive and happy to one that is negative. They then have to separate themselves from the newcomers.

Sadly, these new friends have come from a negative environment, which they themselves would admit wasn't good for them, and moved into a much more positive atmosphere, only in the end to try to take the new friends they have made back to the mentality they used to operate from. In reality they have gone full circle back to where they hated being!

I have noticed lately (thank goodness) that Vanessa has started to distance herself from those friends who only want to be negative. Most of the time, I must add, these friends probably don't even realise that they are being so negative, but unfortunately you can't say anything to them because they get very defensive and put the blame on those around them. I've tried a couple of times, only to be made to feel like the grim reaper, so now I just shut my mouth (it's safer that way).

Who have you got around you who is constantly trying to bring you down to their level? Are you going to let them or are you going to take control over where you want to end up in life and the time it will take you to get there? Sure they will want to be around you while everything is looking good. Success is attractive. But are they going to be around you when you are struggling with issues? I bet not.

Some of you may have had a negative approach to achieving your goals and dreams for many years. This will not change overnight just because you now realise you need to think from a positive perspective. What you will have to work hard at doing is turning those positive thoughts into positive actions, all the time being conscious of the negative mentality that will be telling you that it 'can't be done'—and many times it may seem easier to be negative, to dismiss the positive.

Changing bad habits isn't easy. You have to change thought

processes, patterns, actions and ideas that you have been using for years, maybe even decades. It's much the same as washing a car for the first time after owning it for ten years (heaven forbid!). Think of the amount of dirt and muck that would have built up. It is only after all that dirt is gone that you will see the real car underneath. The effort required to clean that car after all those years will be a lot more than if you only had to clean off one day's worth of dirt. Similarly, once you make the effort to strip away the years of negative thoughts you will see the real you, the one that you can now build onto positive thoughts and actions.

Another step in changing your thinking is understanding that you will at some point in life face disappointments, even failures. Let me give you an example that I saw on television a while ago. I was flicking through the channels (as most males do) and I came across a track-and-field meet. The 400-metre hurdles was just about to start. The athletes lined up, prepared themselves and 'bang', off they went. About halfway through the race one of the competitors caught his foot on a hurdle and knocked it over. He kept on going, however, and finished the race in last place.

I know you are thinking to yourself, 'Not a very interesting story, Justin,' but let me tell you what I got out of that race. All of us at one time or another have been guilty of changing our course purely because we hit a hurdle. Whether it be a new goal or a new business, we were positive when we started, until cold, hard reality hit. We then took the negative way out by changing what we wanted to achieve in the first place (moving the goal posts!) and perhaps even casting blame.

Just like the athletes in the race I watched that day, you need to have the mentality that no matter whether you clear all your hurdles or you knock them all down, you are going to continue in the same direction that you started.

I am yet to watch a hurdles race where an athlete knocks down one of his hurdles, stops, and yells out to his fellow competitors to come back and start again because he feels that it is unfair that he has been disadvantaged. But this is how some of us go through life. As soon as we hit our own hurdles, we expect everyone around us to stop and help us or wait for us to catch up. It doesn't work that way. Life doesn't happen that way.

Having a positive mentality at the start is great, but it is when you are facing challenges that you will really need it to shine. Anyone can give up. It is those who push through the barriers who will reap the rewards in the end.

The last step in changing your thinking from a negative approach to a positive one is to understand what each of these attitudes brings to the party. Negative thinking causes you to hold back; it restricts your ability to reach your goals and dreams; it sets boundaries for you to operate in, by reminding you constantly of 'what didn't work last time'. I am not sure about you but I don't want anything to keep me closed in, especially past failures. I want to achieve so much more in my life and I want to do it in record time. If I am confined by my negative thinking it will be almost impossible for me to achieve half of what I want to achieve.

When you start thinking positively you start breaking down those boundaries. You start seeing how things can be achieved, how goals can be met. There is a sense of hope—you just might end up living one of your dreams. Now I am not talking about being airy-fairy with your thinking—you still need to be realistic; what I am talking about is the ability to see the bigger picture instead of the obstacles that could get in the way.

A simple technique that can help force your thinking towards being positive is to have reminders around your house of what you are trying to achieve. Vanessa every now and then places pictures of things that she would like in our bathroom. Every time she goes in there she can visualise what she is aiming at and then her thinking is focused towards achieving that goal.

There is so much negativity out there in the world—bad news comes at us from all sides. That being the case, make sure you don't add to the load by constantly beating yourself up with negative thoughts.

Be in charge of where you want to end up in life by being in charge of your positive thinking.

2

Understanding what you want out of life

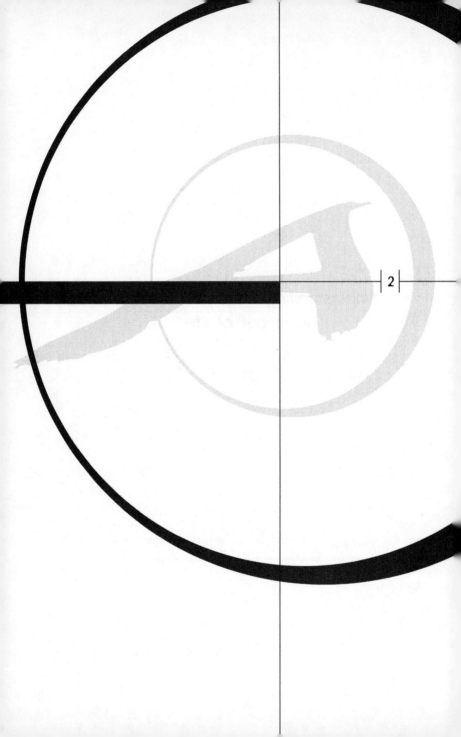

2

There are a lot of people who *think* they know what they want out of their lives—they have this grand plan and big picture—but unfortunately they have no idea at all as to how they are going to achieve any of their goals or dreams.

I believe they really don't know what it is that they actually want. They have a picture of the 'ultimate' goal but that is about it. They cut out pictures from magazines of the big house or the nice car, but still forget that hard work will be required to have those dreams turn into reality. It is the thought of that dream that they like, not so much the realisation of living that dream and the effort that will be required to bring it to life. It will always stay a dream, off in the distance, until they start working towards bringing that goal closer.

Understanding what you actually want out of life is the biggest key to achieving anything in your quest for ultimate happiness. Yes, I know, that statement sounds like common sense, but you would be surprised by the number of people still frustrating themselves on a daily, weekly, monthly, even yearly basis, trying to come to terms with this process.

Too many people don't understand, first, what they want and second, how much effort will be required to get what they desire. You see, it is the effort part that is the biggest key to this whole process. Sure, you may have great goals and dreams, better than anyone else around you. I constantly receive phone calls and letters from people who have some huge goals. But as soon as I explain what will actually be involved in getting them anywhere near their goals, it all becomes 'too hard' and I never hear from them again.

There are so many people today who look at what other people have and think that it was 'easy' for that person to obtain that nice stuff. Then words like 'they are just lucky' start coming out of their mouths. They end up resenting those around them who have achieved, instead of learning from them. Jealousy will be the death of your own dreams and goals if you allow it to infiltrate your thinking and actions.

Luck is not the answer. I believe that you are probably only lucky once or twice on your journey towards achieving those goals and dreams you have set for yourself. Sure, things may come your way, but it is up to you to build upon that luck— for otherwise it will amount to nothing. Luck doesn't last.

There is no guarantee when it comes to luck. A lot of people don't put all their effort into everything they are doing because they are waiting for that 'lucky break' to come along, for the magic fairy who will make all their dreams come true without putting any work or effort in themselves. Some are waiting to win the lottery so they can buy everything that they want, instead of working towards those dreams. The odds are that you will never win the lottery. That being the case, you will fulfil those dreams more quickly by working towards them than by waiting for your numbers to come up.

I use a process which I call 'dumbing life down'. What do I mean by that? We all need to make our lives, goals and dreams as simple as we can. There is no need to have complicated theories and processes in our lives—all that will do is confuse what we are actually trying to achieve and add extra pressure.

We all can get too technical sometimes. We can have one-year plans, five-year plans and even ten-year plans, but some of us still can't get out of bed on time every morning! We end up planning ourselves out of existence with the big stuff and forget about the small issues. The small issues will help us on our way as well, but we tend to overlook them. We seem to think that the small issues just aren't important.

I look at everything that I want to achieve in a way that makes the whole process as simple as it can be just so I can get my head around it. Simplicity is the key to living life. Life is only as complicated as you make it. Some people make things as complicated as they can in an effort to justify to those around them where their own life is actually going and why it is taking them ages to fulfil any of their desires.

The number of people who have sat opposite me in my office with five-year plans that were made ten years ago is amazing. The problem is that they have forgotten to get started, or are too scared to because they are afraid they might fail, so they end up spending all their time planning instead of doing.

Sure, as far as they're concerned everything has been worked out to the finest detail. The problem with that is that it leaves no room for change. They are going about their dreams according to their original plan and have never entertained the thought that there could be a different and easier way to get where they want to go in life. They don't stop and think after a few years or a few disappointments that maybe, just maybe, there is a better way.

You see, you can have a very detailed life plan but still be achieving nothing. What is the point of that? What we all need to see is results. As soon as you see results, you will be encouraged to press on for more results, which will ultimately lead you on to bigger and better things.

Some people are serial dreamers. What I mean by this is that when they don't see any quick results from their goals and dreams, they just keep adding new ones and trying to achieve the new goals, instead of finishing off the original ones. By adding more and more dreams and goals, they think that they are actually achieving something. WRONG!

You see, your dreams and goals are like a jigsaw puzzle. Sure it looks great when it's finished, but when you first start the puzzle it is just one big mess. It isn't until you stop and look at every piece to see where it fits that you will start to see the bigger picture, which takes time, patience and focus.

I don't have a five- or even a ten-year plan. Sure, I know ultimately what I would like to achieve when it comes to my goals, but I am not going to be restricted by a timeline.

I dumb every decision down along the way to make the journey understandable and enjoyable. Everything that I do has to be via the simplest possible method. By doing that I keep the whole process simple and easy to understand. Too much clutter just adds to the mess and, if you are anything like me, you don't really need to add any more mess to your life. Things are bound to go a little left of centre on your journey. That being the case, I need to keep everything simple so I can get things back on track without wasting too much time trying to figure everything out.

What you need to look at is the method required to get you what you want. It is great to know the big picture, the dream or goal that you have written down on a piece of paper. But have you put any thought into what it is going to take to get you there? It is the method that needs the most amount of thought in the whole process. You need to have a plan of attack. There is no point in doing something blindly in the vain hope that everything will work out.

The time and thought that you put into planning how to get to where you want in life will be time well spent. Planning after you have started, and after you have made big mistakes, will be wasted time. I don't want to waste any more time—I did that when I was younger. I want to see results and I want to see them with the least amount of drama possible.

Over the past few years I have been asked to speak to a number of direct marketing organisations across a range of industries. I really like spending time with these groups as the people in them all have one thing in common. They know what they want out of life and, more importantly, they understand what is required to get it. They understand the principle of hard work. They know that their dreams will not just be handed to them.

Sure, everyone has their own opinion of direct marketing, but you cannot deny the results a lot of people achieve within these groups. They are prepared to work hard to get what they want and realise that it is up to them to do it. The successful people in these organisations don't expect other people to carry them to their dreams. They are focused on one thing—fulfilling their dreams themselves, no matter how much effort is required.

The other thing that always amazes me is the amount of passion they have for what they are doing. They understand that while it is great to have a dream, and it is great to work towards that dream, if they don't have a passion for what they are doing then it will all come unstuck and turn into simply another job. The number of successful people within these organisations is astounding—and it's all because they understand exactly what they want out of life and what is required to get it.

Many people know where it is they want to end up with their lives, but unfortunately they fail to plan the method or the journey that will get them there. Let me give you an example. As I am writing this chapter I am sitting at the desk in my office at home. I look out to the kitchen and I can see the cup of coffee that I have just made, but stupidly left in the kitchen. For me to have that coffee in my hot little hands is going to require some effort and action on my part.

That coffee will not come to me; I will have to go to that coffee. So what I need to do is stand up, put one foot in front of the other and make my way from the starting position (my office chair) to the destination (the coffee cup). It is that effort and that action that will result in my gaining the prize. If no effort or action is used to get up and walk over to that cup, then I can only look at myself, not the cup of coffee, as the one to blame for not having it in my hands. No effort = no result; the two go hand in hand.

This is where a lot of people go wrong. They see their goals from their starting position but don't put any effort or action into making their way to the final destination. They think they totally understand what they want out of their lives, and maybe they do, but they fail to understand what will be required to get it. All too often they end up blaming the goal or the dream, when the truth is that they failed to understand what was required to fulfil that desire.

The other unfortunate thing that happens is some of these people who have never reached their goals start despising others who have. It really annoys me when that happens. They are only seeing the end result when they look at other people's success. They rarely see what it took and what it cost to get there. What others have achieved should serve as inspiration for you, not a source of frustration or hindrance.

I have a lot of people wanting to sit down with me to discuss their life and their goals. You would be surprised by the number who ask if I can help them *come up* with some goal or dream. I mean, how the heck would I know what they want to achieve? Yet they still ask with a straight face.

You are the only person who can know where you want to go in your life. We all need to have a sense of ambition, direction and focus. And until you do, you will never achieve anything close to what you desire because you have failed to include some very important ingredients in the mix. Self-realisation and self-understanding need to be placed at the top of your list.

Now don't sit there with a pained expression on your face trying to conjure up a dream. You need to really look at where it is you want to end up, what it is you haven't yet achieved that you have always wanted. You should know without even giving it much thought.

I always remember back to the time I was fifteen and sixteen, when my thinking wasn't clouded with negativity. It was in those years that I set myself some goals without my thinking telling me that they couldn't be achieved.

As we get older our thinking starts to control our actions. We start to believe we can't do something because of all the hurdles we may have to face, instead of just giving it a go as we would have when we were younger. We use every excuse under the sun to justify why not instead of why we should.

Have you got a goal that you've been putting off because you didn't understand what was needed to fulfil it? If so, then get off your backside and move forward. The worst that could happen is that you learn some valuable lessons about yourself.

Once we get to the point of understanding what we want out of our individual lives, we can start living those dreams and making our goals a reality.

Setting your goals | 3 |

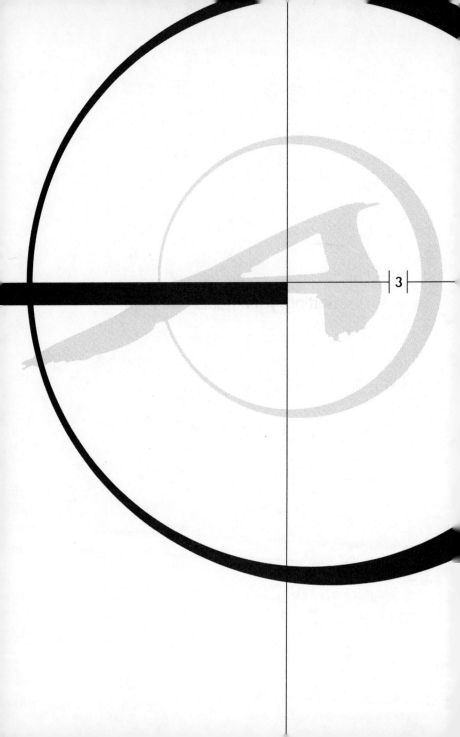

3

Set your goals, write your goals down, look at your goals every day, have a goal. You've all probably heard these bits of advice a million times before.

Unfortunately many of us, even those who have worked out what we want in life, still fail to set ourselves goals, or if we do we fail to check our progress against our listed goals on a regular basis. Without a goal there is no direction. Without direction there is no fulfilment.

When I was 25 and only just starting Attitude Inc.® I had a list of goals. I didn't have many, and I wasn't really sure at the time whether I would achieve any of them, but they were tangible things against which I could measure my progress, and so I made sure I was at least aiming at something.

One of the biggest mistakes that many of us make is to set ourselves goals and dreams that aren't tangible. By that I mean we set goals like 'I want to be rich' or 'I want to be successful'. The problem is you can't reach out and grab or smell this type of goal. They are feelings, emotions, and with emotions come surprises.

Feelings, just like emotions, go up and down. In some sense, they are very difficult to control as they are really at the mercy of what is happening around us instead of what we are making happen. Feelings come and go. Money comes and goes, even success goes up and down.

What you really need to do is set your sights on tangible goals so that once you have reached them you are able to enjoy them, and I mean physically enjoy them. That way there will always be a sense of accomplishment—every time you look or touch that particular goal, you will fully appreciate your efforts, your sweat and hard work.

If one of your goals is to go on a proper holiday with your family once a year, then think about the satisfaction you will feel as you sip cocktails by the hotel pool or watch your kids tumbling down the beginners' slopes at a ski resort. That is the sort of tangible feeling I am talking about, when you can truly appreciate all the hard work and effort it took to get you there.

Another mistake we make when setting goals is that we don't aim far enough away. What I mean by that is that all too often we are guilty of setting goals that are too easy to achieve. This is fine to get ourselves started, but ultimately we need goals and dreams that will push us further than we've ever been pushed before. This, if achieved, will force our thinking and actions on to a new level.

We constantly need to be pushing ourselves. Sure you can have others around you who can push you along, but if you can be the driving force in achieving those goals, then the degree of satisfaction you feel at the completion of those dreams will be worth the effort—because you will know it was you who got you there and no-one else.

At the age of 25 I was yet to understand this principle. My only goal seemed to be just getting through the week with enough money. I didn't think about the future. It wasn't that I was never taught the principle of goal-setting. I think it was that I didn't believe that I would ever be able to achieve any goals I set. So I did what most people do: I didn't bother having any. I was just going to let life happen to me instead of making my own life. I was willing to do whatever felt good at the time, hoping that it would work out to something bigger. Yes, yes, yes, I was totally mistaken.

The day I decided that I was sick and tired of not achieving anything was the first week into my business. I wanted the nice stuff that other people around me had. The time of blaming everyone else for my lack of accomplishment had come to an end.

So in that first week I sat down and wrote out my goals. I kept my list very short—there were only three. I didn't want to confuse myself so I made it as simple as I could. As I said in my first book, you are the one who sets your standards, which in turn makes you responsible for the outcome. That being the case, I didn't want to set myself up to fail so I made the process as simplistic and as structured as I could.

I believe it is a big mistake to write down heaps and heaps of goals. Doing this may make you feel you have a purpose, but it may also overwhelm you. Achieving your goals should be a pleasure, not a pressure so intense that it sends you loopy due to the inevitable feelings of lack of accomplishment.

What I did was write down my goals in the order that I needed to achieve them. A lot of people write down their list of goals and dreams with no thought of the order in which they need to be accomplished. They have a big goal here, a small goal next, then another big goal, and so on. The problem with doing this is that there is no logic to the progression—you are not forcing yourself or pushing yourself to be better and bigger each time you move on.

My first goal

My first goal was just to prove to someone that she was wrong about me. It may sound like a silly goal to you, but you might be surprised by what you first need to achieve before moving on to the bigger stuff.

Sometimes the first things we need to achieve may seem irrelevant to others, but they are hugely relevant to our own journey. For some of you reading this book, your first goal may be to prove something to yourself. If you can't convince yourself that you can do it, you have no chance of convincing others.

After being successful in the start-up of my business I knew that I had proved my point and achieved my first goal. The person I wanted to prove wrong had to know that she might have misjudged me. If she didn't, at least I had proved to myself that I had more in me than a lot of people would have given me credit for.

Now I could have not bothered trying to prove anything to this person, and either ignored her continuous negative comments or answered back with remarks like 'You don't know anything about me' or 'You are so wrong about me', but I felt this wouldn't have had any impact on myself. Those comments, had I made them, might have made me feel a little better for a short time, but I wanted to move on so I had to address the perceptions behind them once and for all.

My second goal

One of my next goals, as explained in my first book, was a personal one, to own a nice car. For you it may be something else, like enjoying more time with your family or going on a holiday. Your goals are your goals; don't let others judge you on their worthiness. There are probably a few people who think my goals were silly. That's fine, I don't live their life, I live mine. That being the case, I am going to use whatever methods I can that will take me to greater heights within my own life.

Which brings me to a side point. Don't ever let others judge as to whether what you want out of your life is right or wrong. Only you know what you want, so go for it. My whole theory is, if a 'silly' goal got me to where I am today, then who is the smarter one?

I always liked and admired nice fast cars, but I had (up until that time) resigned myself to the fact that I would never have one. So I set about fulfilling that desire once and for all. It took me two years before I could purchase my dream car at the time. I have to say the feelings that I had when I sat in that car made the years of dreaming so much more worthwhile.

Then I decided to go for the 'ridiculous' goal.

My third goal

A 'ridiculous' goal is the big one you just throw in at the end of the list, the one you 'know' you will never achieve, but seeing that you are writing the list you throw it in there anyway while caught up in the excitement.

My 'ridiculous' goal was that I wanted to 'retire', to have my business fully operational, to create a business that was a great passive income stream, by the time I was 31 years old. That would give me the freedom to pursue anything else I desired without having to worry about the financial implications.

At the time I wrote this goal down, I wasn't even sure if I would last to the next week with my business, let alone the next year. As soon as I reached the goal of owning my first dream car, I started to think about that huge dream that I'd set for myself just two years earlier. Until I reviewed that original list, I had totally forgotten that I had written it down.

You see I didn't get caught up in continually looking at all the goals I first listed. If I'd done that I would have been focusing on too many things at the one time. All I would have achieved would have been confusion.

Focus on one goal at a time

It was easier for me to then focus on that huge dream because of the successful completion of the goals I had previously set. I now was able to focus my attention on that huge goal. My sights were firmly placed on achieving it; the fact that nothing else would cloud my vision really helped me with my focus. I was able to achieve that goal within my original timeframe because first, I made sure that I focused on one goal at a time, and second, I made sure that the next goal was a bigger challenge.

Stretch yourself

I have many theories. Those who know me well know that I have an opinion on just about everything. One of the theories that I now live by is the process of setting and achieving my own goals at higher and higher levels.

You see, too often we set ourselves only the same level of goal all the time. We know how much effort is required to reach that level and just plod along without stretching ourselves further. Sure, we might achieve our goals time after time, but what we don't experience is the growth that comes with stretching ourselves to reach greater heights.

After reaching my huge goal (the one I just tacked on to the end of the list, that I never thought I would reach), I decided to take a different approach. Now every time I reach a goal I've set for myself I replace it with a bigger one. Then when that one is fulfilled I replace it with an even bigger one again. This way I am constantly growing, constantly forcing myself to greater heights. If I didn't do this, I wouldn't be challenging myself and I would end up becoming stagnant and bored with my life and its outcomes.

What is it that you have been trying to reach? Are you sure that you have set your goals correctly? Maybe you have set your first goal or dream so far off in the distance that it is making you question whether you want to keep aiming at it.

Start off by visualising yourself completing that first goal. Your sense of achievement at fulfilling that goal will spur you on to wanting to achieve more. There is nothing like success in something to push you on to greater things.

Your future and your dreams and goals are exactly that—YOURS. So, what are you waiting for?

4

Dream big!

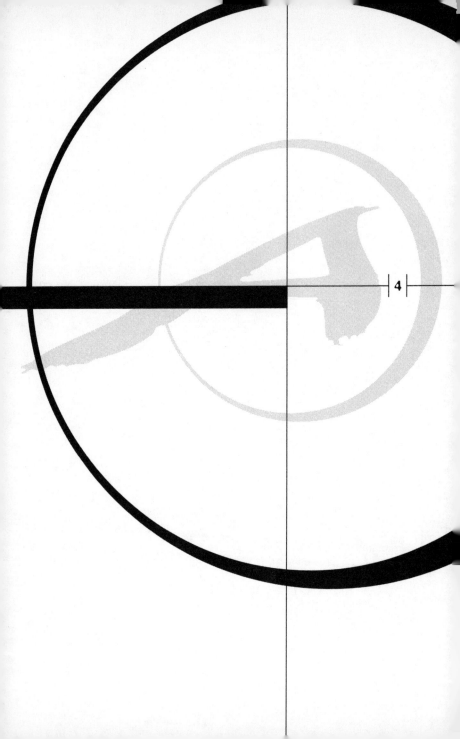

From the first day of my business I had dreams. They weren't huge, just dreams that I was sure I would be able to achieve one day. I had the idea that if I didn't want to fail I would have to keep my dreams within reach. I was wrong in not setting out to stretch myself as well—but this is a mistake many people make in the beginning.

By the end of the first year my whole perception had changed. I began to realise the bigger the dream, the bigger the outcome. It had to be beyond easy reach. But with that comes the bigger the dream, the bigger the sacrifice. What I had to do, and quickly, was rethink my entire dream plans.

In that first year I had many challenges. One of the major challenges was to change my way of thinking. If I was to reach those big dreams that I had now set myself, I had to radically change the way I thought. We all want to change direction at some point in our lives but many of us don't address our thinking at the same time. This means we go about trying to achieve new things using old attitudes.

In the beginning I was plodding along handling sales of one or two t-shirts at a time. While there were many orders of this kind, I knew that there was a quicker way to success but I was yet to discover it.

I wanted the bigger sales. I wanted the type of sales that would bring my dreams into reality a lot faster. The key to bigger sales wasn't selling more; it was expanding my dreams to wanting better stuff, wanting to achieve more. Expanding what I wanted to achieve forced me to step up to the plate to get the results that were needed. I had to change the focus of my dream.

One of my dreams was to be on television as a reporter. Yes I know, nothing big, but I really enjoyed the challenge it set me—and one day I was asked to be a reporter for a small business show. This was a great opportunity, as I could reach the small-business people with great business principles on a national scale—something I had really wanted to achieve.

One of the first stories I did was a story on defensive driving. This was a great story for me, as it was really in line with my passion for cars. One of the principles the driving instructors pointed out was that of focus. The majority of drivers keep their vision too close to the front of the vehicle. It is when you raise your line of sight and look further into the distance that you are able to see a lot more and in turn react a lot more quickly. When you look further ahead, your peripheral vision still takes in the car in front, but you see so much more than that.

I believe that there are many people who are so focused on the easy goals and the short-term dreams that they are not seeing the bigger picture. When they raise their sights to encompass the whole picture, they will be able to complete everything that they want while still heading in the correct direction. That is because their vision is now wider, and so are their prospective outcomes.

After the first year of Attitude Inc.®, my ultimate dream was to have a worldwide brand. I wasn't shy. I wanted it all. Now in reality there was absolutely no way I could afford financially, let alone manage, what I wanted at that time. What I could do, though, was start to prepare myself for the future I was looking towards.

You see, you will have your big dreams. They will always be there. But it is from the successes of achieving your smaller dreams that the lessons and methods will be learnt to achieve those monster dreams. It all comes down to what you are focused on. If all you focus on is the small tasks right in front of you, then that is all you will ever accomplish. Because I moved my focus from directly in front of me, lifted it up and away from me, I was able to see a lot more clearly. I was able to see the bigger picture for my life. I was able to finally understand what I was trying to achieve.

Let me demonstrate this in a more practical way. Place the palm of your hand close to your nose. What do you see? Probably just a blur of skin. Now slowly pull your hand away from your face until your arm is stretched out straight. Now what do you see? You will see a hand with five fingers on the end of it.

It is that clarity that we need when it comes to focusing on our goals and dreams. We are all guilty of aiming at the easy goals directly in front of our faces; you know, the ones that don't really require much effort. What we need to have are dreams and goals that are out of reach but still within focus. The further away the better. That way you will be continually focused on them until you achieve them. Make sure, though, that you don't give up, that you don't fall into the trap of thinking that it is all too hard. Push through that mental barrier—the reward may be just around the corner.

We all need to be like a dog with a bone. We own a Staffordshire bull terrier called Diesel. Diesel is a great dog. When we give him a bone he is in doggy heaven. He loves his bone so much that there is absolutely no way that you or I could get it off him, no matter how hard we might try. He locks his jaw on that bone and refuses to give it up.

Be like a dog with a bone with your dreams. Refuse to give them up, no matter who or what comes along to take them from you. It may even be you who tries to give up your dreams. Don't. Keep hold of them until they are completed and you are living what you had desired from the start. Develop a 'lockjaw' mentality with what you want to achieve.

As I said at the start of this chapter, I began with small goals, things that were within reach. Please do not misunderstand me when I say I was wrong. You need small dreams and goals to start with, because achieving them will provide very valuable lessons that will help you reach towards the bigger dreams, the things just out of reach.

When you achieve any goal the feelings of joy and accomplishment will be quite evident. It is those feelings that are needed to help you understand the rewards that you will get when accomplishing the next dream.

Too many people underestimate the area of feelings. We think sometimes that it is not good to express happiness if we have achieved something spectacular because we don't want to upset those around us who aren't doing so well. What a joke! We need to show excitement. We need to let loose sometimes.

The days that I operated really well were the days when something good had happened and made me feel great. It was that feeling that spurred me on to greater things. With that, you also need to understand that if things don't work out for you, sometimes you won't be feeling the best. You need to remember those bad feelings as a guide to what not to do in the future. The key is to not let those 'off' days affect you in a negative way. Use every experience, every outcome for the positive.

So what are 'big dreams'? We are constantly told to 'dream big' but for many of us that seems too pie-in-the-sky type stuff. Some people's interpretation of dreaming big is making stupid decisions and just hoping that things work themselves out. They think that a big dream gives them the right to stop using their brains and just do whatever they want, whatever they feel needs to be done.

Well, in reality, what needs to occur when it comes to working towards those big dreams is that you need to be at the smartest point of your life. You need to have your wits about you. You need to operate in a different way, to think on a different level. You have to change the way that you approached your last dream or goal.

One of your big dreams may be to own a huge house

outright. Now if you are careless about fulfilling this dream then you will probably go in the opposite direction. Let me explain. You may want a big house one day and you may want to pay for it outright as that is your ultimate dream. So you start working towards fulfilling that dream. After a while you get impatient, so to speed things along you decide that instead of waiting until you have the money to buy that house, you'll skip a few months, if not years, and take out a loan.

Some of you reading may even think that isn't such a bad move. BUT: What happens if things start to die off with your work? What happens if unforeseen circumstances arise, causing you to struggle with meeting those payments? And they are huge payments because it was a huge dream.

You see, by trying to speed up your dreams by taking short cuts, all you are potentially doing is forcing yourself backwards. All you have looked at is the end result. You have failed to look at the method required, the original plan (buying it outright) or to consider the personal cost that will result from things going a little pear-shaped.

I don't want or need added pressure when it comes to living my dreams. There is enough pressure out there without my own stupidity being thrown in the mix. Just as in the house example, I am the only one who can help or hinder the living of my dreams.

Yes, of course, I want to have that nice house just like everybody else. The difference with me is that I want to own that house outright before I move in. That is my 'big goal'. If I have a goal, then I want to stick to it as much as I can. As soon as

I change the rules, I am potentially changing the outcome, which takes away my control of the dream. (Now I am not saying for a minute that you shouldn't get a loan for your house, so don't get your knickers in a knot. I am just using the house as an example of the need not to change the rules as you go along. Phew.)

Remember, your big goals need to be way out of reach. If they are really easy to achieve then there isn't much of a challenge. Without the challenge there won't be that much accomplished, because of the limited focus. Sure, I could go and get a loan for that house. And yes, I could most probably live in that house with no problems and eventually pay it off. But imagine the feelings of satisfaction the day you move into that house debt-free. Imagine what impetus that will give to fulfilling your other goals and dreams. You have just created your own benchmark.

Just because I reach one of my goals doesn't mean I should then stop. This is where a lot of people get mixed up. They only have a couple of things that they want to achieve. They still think that success is a destination. Once those few goals have been completed, and there are no new ones to aim for, they become directionless. They are then at the mercy of life, allowing life to happen around them with no control over where they will end up.

Every time you fail to fulfil your goals and dreams, you are forcing yourself back into your comfort zone. Not only that, your comfort zone gets smaller and smaller with each unmet goal or dream.

Don't set yourself up for failure by trying to speed things up because you have just figured out that reaching your goal will require a lot of time and effort. That's just a band-aid solution. All you are doing then is aiming for the end feeling rather than life-long satisfaction. Understand that to complete big dreams—not little ones—will take time and focused effort. As I have said before, if it was easy to live your dreams then EVERYBODY would be living them.

One of the biggest keys to fulfilling not only the big dreams but also the small dreams is the process of visualisation. Now don't get freaked out—I am not talking about some wacky process. I mean that unless we can see in our minds what we are trying to achieve, the goal is going to be a lot harder to reach. It will end up being just an idea, not a reality.

My younger brother Dean has always been good at applying this principle. He has always had pictures of houses, cars and anything else that he has wanted up around his office. Not too long ago Dean and his wife Bernice moved into their new home. I have to say, I normally view houses as houses, but this house is spectacular. This is the house that they have always dreamed of. It didn't happen overnight for them, but through hard work and the process of working through their smaller dreams and goals they have managed to achieve what was totally out of reach a few years ago.

Recently I was in the garage at Dean's new home and I noticed an outline of a car drawn on the floor. I asked him what it was for. Dean told me that his next big dream was to own a Porsche Boxter. He asked someone who owned one to come over and he traced the outline of that Porsche onto the garage floor.

Dean will not allow any other car to park in that space. He is visualising that car parked in his garage one day, and until it is there nothing will take its place. At the time of writing this book I know that Dean is only months away from parking the real car in that space.

You see, when you have your dreams in your mind and you are thinking of them all the time, it is not easy to forget them. When you can't forget something you will be continually reminded of it, and when you are reminded of something it is easier to put into action.

The last thought that I want to leave you with on the subject of dreaming big is starting small. You will never live the big dreams if you can't fulfil the small dreams along the way. I know some people who only have huge dreams. That is great for their egos, but unfortunately, because they don't understand that the small dreams must be accomplished first, they will always fail to get anywhere near the big ones.

You need to be faithful to the little things before you can accomplish the big. Work your way up with your dreams. Have your huge dreams, but get to them by using the smaller dreams as stepping-stones. I would not be sitting here today with an internationally licensed brand if I hadn't sold that first shirt. Remember, it isn't how fast you can live your dreams, it is how long you live them that matters.

What you are able to accomplish in your life is only limited by how big you can dream.

Passion is an action

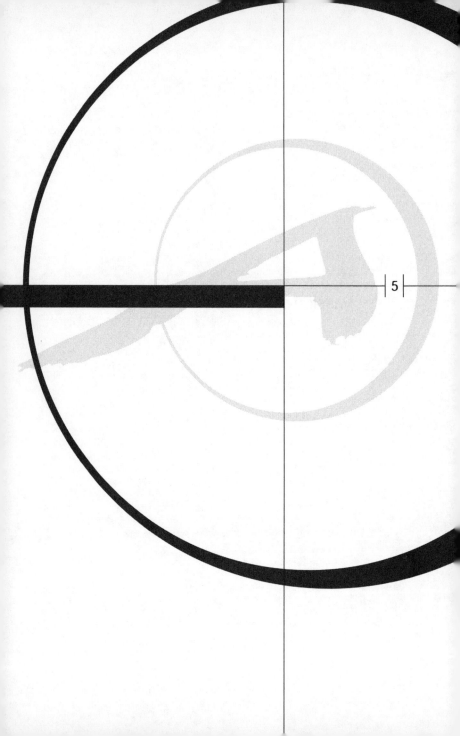

5

Passion is a word that seems to get thrown around all the time these days—so much so that I feel sometimes it loses its real meaning and impact. Without passion, however, I would never have fulfilled my desires. Passion is the fuel that you need to get you to your goals and dreams. Just like a car, without fuel you go nowhere. And if you put the wrong fuel in, or you put cheap fuel in, you will not perform to your full potential.

This chapter is all about understanding what the ingredients are for the fuel (passion) that you need to put into your goals and dreams so you can perform and reach your fullest potential. I want to show you the areas that make up passion by breaking the word down letter by letter:

Productivity
Awareness
Sensitivity
Sowing
Individuality
Ownership
Not negotiable.

The reason behind this is that without knowing what is required to get to our goal, sometimes we tend to either dismiss or overlook the results that could be gained. If we look at things too simply, we will only get a small percentage of their value from them. I want you to understand what makes up passion. Then it can be part of every aspect of your life.

Remember, passion is more than just a word that sounds good. It should be part of who you are. It is an action; it needs to be acted upon.

Productivity

Passion is great as a word, but without being productive it will remain just that—A WORD! Productivity requires a whole lot of action. It is that action that will produce results. There are many people out there who have great dreams and a long list of goals, and claim to be 'passionate' about achieving them, but who are too lazy to get off their backsides to make it all happen. As soon as hard work and effort are required, they back off into their own world of laziness.

Without being productive, those dreams you have will just stay in the distance, never coming any closer to reality. Passion, I believe, produces more passion. As you start to use your passion in whatever you are doing or whatever you are trying to achieve, it will first, start to grow your dream into bigger and wider areas, and second, open your eyes to possibilities which you may not have even contemplated, bringing on a sense of further accomplishment. You start seeing the finish line to your goals and dreams, which gives you an understanding of why you have been doing what you have been doing.

I was so passionate about starting up my clothing company that all I slept and breathed was Attitude Inc.®. While that was great, it wasn't until I was productive that anything eventuated. Which in turn made more doors open, and made me even more passionate about what I had set out to do in the first place.

I could have talked your ears off about what I was going to achieve. Talk is cheap, anyone can talk, but it is the action that goes with that talk that will bring results in the end.

Stop talking about your goals. Stop giving 'lip service' to them, as one of my friends would say. Be productive with what you want and where you want to end up. Act upon those desires.

Awareness

Being aware of what is happening around you may sound like common sense, but it would probably surprise you if you knew how many people miss the boat. As I said earlier, there are many opportunities out there that, if taken, may get you to your goals and dreams just that little bit quicker. Some people have everything planned out to the smallest detail but they miss fantastic opportunities that could have made that journey a whole lot simpler, purely by overplanning and under-performing.

Having the big picture is important, but you need to make small steps first to get there. I have met numerous people who have told me that 'years ago I had a great idea, but I didn't act upon it until it was too late, or I didn't act upon it at all'. This, I believe, is because they were not aware of the opportunities that were there in front of them. It is too late to wish that you 'should have' or you 'could have' when it comes to your dreams. Being aware of what is happening around you and what could happen is what being passionate is all about.

Awareness is just the start of the process; action following that awareness is what's really important. Knowing what is out there, knowing what opportunities there are in front of you is one thing, but acting upon them is what it is all about.

As passion will open up new doors and opportunities that you may never have thought of, you need to be fully alert and aware that these things may and will happen. Stop doing things the same way you've always done them. Be aware of new ways of trying things, of new methods, or even of the different people you need to be around—all these things will stretch you to fulfil those goals and dreams.

Be observant, be aware of the areas in your life that need attention. Look for the little things that keep popping their heads up every time you try to complete a goal, things that squash your passion and drive. It is those little things that you need to be aware of.

Remember, most of the time it is the little things we aren't aware of that can destroy our journey before we even get started. It is great that we are looking out for new and exciting methods, and areas where we can reach our goals and dreams, but we also need to be aware of those areas that are keeping us from reaching them—our attitudes, our thinking and even those around us.

Sensitivity

If you ask anyone close to me (my wife included), they will quickly tell you that I am not a very sensitive person. This is something that I am working on every day. I am more of a 'just get over it' type of guy. I can't stand whingers and I especially can't stand people who have every excuse under the sun as to why they 'haven't succeeded yet'.

This has had to change after having children, as 'just get over it' doesn't work that well when there are bumps and bruises happening every five minutes. It is the same when it comes to the passion level that I put into achieving my own goals and dreams. I need to have a sensitivity to how much passion is required.

Let me explain. Have you ever heard the expression 'like a bull in a china shop'? This is how some people come across with their expressed passion. They are in your face and full on to the point of annoyance. It ends up turning you right off being around them, as it all appears too fake and too much.

The level of your passion for what you want to do is entirely up to you. But don't thrust your passion in people's faces; it can be very off-putting to those who are yet to reach where you are at personally. All that will do is create an environment of resentment, which is the last thing I want to do. I don't want people to resent me, I want to uplift and encourage those I come in contact with. That then requires a level of sensitivity to their needs, not mine.

You see, reaching and fulfilling all that you want out of life isn't about making those around you feel less than you. Most people are made to feel like that on a daily basis. Your accomplishments, if anything, should encourage others to lift themselves to greater heights. Being sensitive with your display of passion is not only a strength that is essential, it is also a skill that when learnt and mastered will be an asset, one of the factors to your success.

Sowing

Have you ever thought about how fruit and vegetables get into the stores and then onto our dinner plates? While we all like the produce (not so much myself, I am more of a meat type of guy), there is one step that if left out would stop the whole process happening.

That step is the sowing of the seed. The farmers have to place that seed in the ground before any products appear on your plate. I know what you are thinking: 'That's not a new and fantastic fact, Justin.' Think about it, though—it is one action that produces many rewards. It is the passion that you put into your efforts that will grow your dreams into real-life existence. It is that first seed you sow in your mind that could turn out to produce a great harvest, but only if you water it with passion.

A percentage of the farmers' seeds never grows. Some of those seeds never make it to harvest. There is a lesson here for us as well. Just because you are passionate about something does not necessarily mean that your goal will come to life.

I don't think the farmers cry over the small percentage that is lost. They keep harvesting those crops that have grown, knowing that once they have harvested they will then need to re-plant. If something doesn't work for you, don't lose sleep over it and don't throw in the towel. Move on to the things that are working for you. Make sure you have other goals and dreams that you are ready to sow. As I keep saying, if everything worked for everyone, then the whole world would be full of successful people all living their goals and dreams.

It is fine to have more passion than is really needed, but without sowing your dream, planting it, watering it and harvesting it, it will never become a reality. Like the farmers who have to get up early in the morning and work on their crops, so do you need to work constantly on your potential harvest: your dreams and goals. Don't forget, though, your dreams are just seeds until you water them with your passion.

Individuality

You are who you are. What makes you tick, what makes you think, what drives you, is all you. It is that same you who has the potential to make your goals and dreams come to life. Ultimately, you are who you are, good and bad. It is up to you to be the best you can be.

Too many times people start changing when they reach some level of success in life. In some instances the person they were starts changing for the worse. Being your own person is extremely important along your journey in life.

I know a guy who has become quite famous recently. While he has experienced some level of success over the years, it was nothing compared to where he is right now. The problem I have is that he has changed. He no longer is the person who had dreams and goals, he is now more concerned with being like everybody else around him. He now prefers to 'fit in' to the crowd he associates with instead of keeping his individuality (the same individuality that got him to where he is today). His growth has become stunted. It is a real pity as he has yet to reach his full potential.

Your passion can disappear as quickly as it comes if you are not careful. You shouldn't alter the level of passion needed in your life unless it is in a positive direction. Too many people make the big mistake of reducing their passion levels as soon as they reach one of their goals or dreams. If only they realised that it was the passion of wanting to achieve that got them to where they are, and that in reality the same (if not more) passion is required to achieve even more.

No matter where you end up—fulfilling your dreams or working on them—remember to remain the real you.

The number of people these days who try to make me change is unbelievable, especially in the area of my speaking. I seem always to be getting 'advice' from the 'professionals' as to how I need to add things to my presentation, or 'maybe wear a suit, Justin'. On the other hand, I currently get around 80 emails a day from other people who have either read my book or heard me speak. The one thing that comes up constantly in those emails is that I am so real. They love that I am me in everything that I do, from the way I speak to the way I dress (not that it is bad, I might add, I just don't like suits that much).

You see, I could change everything for those so-called 'experts'. But it is the people who I am trying to reach that I care about. And from where I stand, they are pretty happy with the individuality that I show. They are happy with me the way I am.

Be you, don't change for others just because they tell you to. I speak about this at length in Chapter 7, but here I am talking about being true to yourself. There will always be knockers out there trying to change you from being you. But it is your individuality that makes you, you.

Ownership

It seems to me that there is a lack of ownership these days in achieving our own goals. People seem to be using other people to reach their goals instead. Whatever you have set for yourself to achieve, whether it be a personal goal or a business goal, you need to own the dream right from the start.

There is an old saying that is still used today, 'easy come, easy go'. This, unfortunately, is how some people accept their fate when it comes to their goals and dreams. It is all too easy to write down a list of goals without taking ownership over completing any of them.

I had a man around 40 years old come up to me recently after I had spoken at a conference who was upset as he now saw that it was he who was to blame for where he was in his life, not others around him. Now I was not sure exactly what I had said, but it must have been what he needed to hear at the time. He had been more about blaming others for his lack of accomplishment than about taking ownership of where he was in his own life path—which had been the easy path to take, the one of least resistance.

Passion is great, but prolonged passion will eventually lead to fulfilment of dreams and goals ONLY if you take ownership of your direction right from the start. I guarantee that you'll take ownership of your achievements if everything works out the way you want it to. That being the case, you need to own the journey from the start—all of it, not just the good results.

Not negotiable

I am not sure if you have the two words 'not negotiable' printed across your cheques, but whether you do or not you need to look at these two words in a different light, as an element of passion. In layman's terms, 'not negotiable' means that no-one but the person or company whose name is written on the cheque can put that money into their account. It is a pity that so few people adopt the principle of 'not negotiable' for their dreams and goals.

Why is it that we are all guilty of allowing others to affect our passion, our goals and the dreams that we have set for ourselves? I believe that as soon as you allow others around you to affect the level of your passion, you instantly allow them (by default) to dictate the outcome of your goals and dreams.

If you fail to put 'not negotiable' on your cheque, you are essentially allowing the drawer of that cheque to change the details. The same principle applies to your dreams. You have now given open permission, while you may not have consciously agreed to it, for anyone to overwrite your grand plan. I am not sure about you, but sometimes it is hard enough trying to keep focused on achieving your own goals and dreams without someone else having a say in the matter!

As you can see, passion is more than just a word. Passion is something that, if understood fully, will launch you into the great world of your goals and dreams. Guard your dreams and goals. Use your passion level as a guide to how much you really want those goals to become a reality. Don't underestimate passion. Just as it brings great rewards when applied, it also leaves big holes if not applied.

Be passionate, not only about where you want to end up in life—be passionate about life itself.

There's no such word as 'can't'

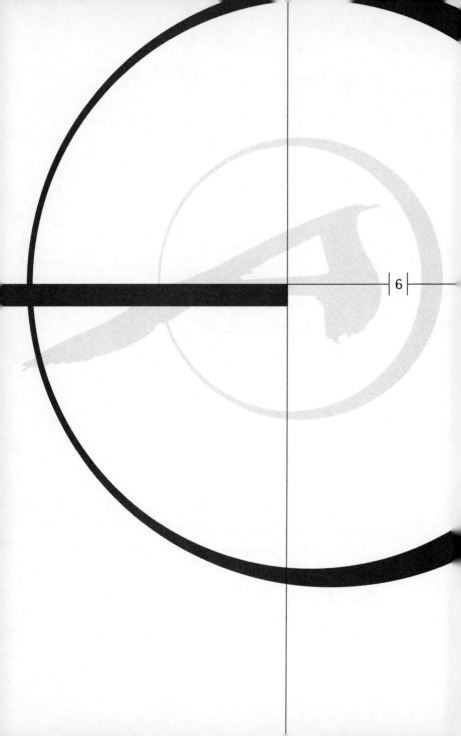

6

I remember a few years ago I was given a framed picture as a gift after speaking at a sales conference. This picture was of a car driving along a long road winding down a steep mountain, with a caption underneath that read: 'A bend in the road is not the end of the road unless you fail to make the turn.' This is now how I view every situation and venture that I enter into. No matter whether it is in my personal life or my business life, I apply that statement to my journey.

How many people do you know (maybe even yourself) who, as soon as something difficult crosses their path, give up? All they see are the bends in the journey instead of the straight road at the foot of their mountain—even worse, they come out with the words 'I CAN'T'.

Can't is an excuse. We all at some time in our lives use excuses to justify our direction or lack of accomplishment. The problem with this is that we eventually start believing the excuses we come up with. Then we start operating from a point of those 'facts' that not long ago were just the excuses we used to make us feel justified in our new and mistaken direction.

The reason I want to discuss this is that most times we think 'can't' means that something just cannot be achieved, end of argument, no correspondence will be entered into. When people use the can't excuse, I believe they are really saying one or more of the following four things: I don't want to, I'm too lazy, I couldn't be bothered, or it's not the right time. Let me expand on each one.

I don't want to

This is a conscious thought process. By saying this you are admitting to yourself that really you don't want to move in the direction that you were heading. It may be the right answer for some of you reading this right now—perhaps you have been heading down the wrong path, aiming at something that you really don't want.

For others, it may be the excuse that you use all the time as soon as things start getting tough. You may be expecting your dreams and goals to happen easily, that the effort required is just much more than you are willing to put in. This is a real shame because with real effort comes real results.

You probably come into contact every day with people who would fit into this category. While they want everything that life has to offer, they too easily get to a point where it all becomes too hard, resulting in their giving up. They may even try to justify their lack of achievement by blaming others, but the real reason for their failings is that they just don't want it badly enough.

I'm too lazy

Laziness is basically lack of appropriate action. Without action there is absolutely no way that you will ever reach those goals you have set for yourself. Some people actually believe that one day they will reach their goals and live their dreams without lifting a single finger. Being lazy is probably the worst mindset to overcome; it has the potential to affect every part of your life and lifestyle. It can become way too easy to justify every reason why you haven't achieved anything without ever admitting to yourself that it comes down to pure laziness. You will know if this is you as soon as you have finished this point.

As I just said, laziness is lack of action. That being the case, turn your actions around. Understand that until you change, nothing will change.

I have a friend who has so much potential that it is scary. He has the best business ideas, and if only he would get off his backside things would happen for him in a big way. The problem he faces is that he is too lazy. He is waiting for everybody else to fulfil his dreams. He has now reached the point where no-one wants to get involved with him, because we all know that we will end up doing all the work while he takes the glory.

The biggest problem lazy people have is that most of them don't realise that they are lazy. In effect they short-circuit their goals by being blind to their own faults.

I couldn't be bothered

This is an attitudinal issue. Between this and 'I'm too lazy', it's probably better to admit to this one—not that many people do.

When 'I couldn't be bothered' is the real reason behind not moving towards your goals, all you need to do is change your thinking to a more positive outlook. You cannot put blame on anyone or any circumstance when this is the true reason. It is up to you and only you to change this type of mentality.

It's not the right time

I am yet to meet someone who doesn't want to experience some level of success in his or her life. But I have met many people who think that it is all too hard and so they don't even give it a try. The first step is starting something that could take you closer to your dreams. Waiting for the 'perfect time' is a waste of time.

Today is the perfect time to start. Stop procrastinating and stop being your own personal and negative nightmare.

It is the can'ts in our lives, our thinking and our actions that stop or hinder our progress. We build up walls around our thinking and actions that eventually inhibit our outcomes. Every time you say you can't do something, you train your mind to accept a lesser option. That in turn will become a habit of always falling short of your goals.

I have a slogan t-shirt that says, 'Nobody trains for second best'. I am yet to watch a race where the runner-up turns around and says that finishing in second position was exactly where they wanted to finish. It just doesn't happen. They all go out there to win.

What we need to do is instil a mindset, the determination to finish our race and to finish in first place. The race I am referring to doesn't involve others, it is our race against our own thinking and negativity. It is the race of life and living it to the fullest with the ultimate results—our results.

Remember, though, you don't get any extra points for achieving your goals and dreams in record time. If you are too impatient you face the risk of taking short-cuts that may end up costing you your dream.

A great mate of mine, Brett, summed it up really well during a discussion regarding this chapter. He said, 'Excuses are like armpits, everybody's got a couple and they both stink.' While that paints a somewhat horrible mental picture he has a great point. Excuses are never a reason as to why you 'can't' reach your goals and dreams. Excuses will only force you further down a path leading away from where you eventually want to end up, all the time creating a false sense of justification as to why you haven't reached anything yet.

When you use excuses as the reason why you can't reach a goal that you've set for yourself, you are basically stopping before you have even started. You have barely made a baby step along your journey. You have only looked at the foot of the mountain instead of seeing its peak.

Let me give you some common statements (or excuses) that you may relate to:

- 'There's not enough time in the day for me to spend quality time with my family because I am working hard to provide for them.'
- 'I haven't got enough qualifications to start my own business.'

- 'It's too hard to save for a home deposit.'
- 'Everybody else gets the promotions at work but I get overlooked all the time for no reason.'

All these excuses are just one-eyed, one-dimensional, slanted views on a situation. Many people out there are fulfilling their goals and dreams every day. Sure, some of them *may*, and I do emphasise may, have started in a better position than you, but there are many thousands of people on this planet who've succeeded in reaching their goals who were in the same position, if not a worse one, than you are in right now. It is easy to excuse our failings by comparing ourselves with others. That, I believe, is one of the biggest mistakes some people make.

It all comes down to changing your mentality towards achieving what you want out of life, as well as just how hard you are willing to fight for it.

Nothing is impossible—have a 4-minute mile mentality

In the early 1950s the biggest challenge for any track-and-field runner was to break the 4-minute mark for running a mile. This was a goal that no-one seemed to be able to reach. It had eluded runners for many years.

Then in 1954 a man by the name of Roger Bannister cracked it. He ran the mile in 3 minutes and 59.4 seconds. For weeks, months and even years beforehand, many had tried but failed to reach that magical time. Seeing that Roger Bannister was the first in history to do it, you might have expected his world record would have stood for quite some time. Well, the thing that shocked me when I found out was that there were numerous athletes, some say over 50 runners that same year, who all ran under the 4-minute mark after Roger Bannister's achievement.

The 4-minute mile was a mental barrier. Once it was shown that it could be done, it opened up the floodgates to everybody else who had been trying to give it a shot. The bar had been set before the record was broken, but as soon as the record fell a new benchmark was set. You need to address where your benchmark is every day. To get a better result tomorrow, you will need to clear the bar that you set for yourself yesterday.

I keep a saying in my wallet: 'The impossible is what no-one can do until somebody does it.' This was true in the case of the 4-minute mile. What is it that you think is so impossible that you are not willing to give it a go? What 'can't' you see yourself completing? What is it that is blurring your vision so that all you see are the reasons why you can't instead of why you can?

If you haven't achieved those goals and dreams that you have been trying to reach for years, it's time to approach them in a different manner. Stop looking at why you haven't been able to fulfil them and concentrate on what you need to do to get there.

As I was born in 1970, I wasn't around when the first man landed on the moon. I can just imagine the comments and ridicule when the idea of attempting this amazing feat was first put forward. I can guarantee you that there would have been more than the odd 'you can't do that' remark. I could also guarantee that the word 'impossible' was thrown in on numerous occasions.

The moon landing, I would say, would have to be one of the biggest events in the history of our planet. All from an initial idea that turned into an amazing reality that had a huge impact worldwide on people's thinking. What is your 'man on the moon' dream or goal? Why can't you achieve and live it? It is entirely up to you to reach your goal. By saying 'can't' you are already admitting to yourself that you cannot see the end result, you cannot see yourself achieving your goals and dreams. You have just become short-sighted; what you are focusing on are the short-term problems and the short-term hurdles instead of the bigger picture. You have put up a wall that will continue to block your vision until you knock it down.

Remember the saying 'where there's a will there's a way'? It is so true. If you want something strongly enough, you will achieve it no matter what stands in your way. What we all need to do (and this may sound a little rah rah) is replace the word 'can't' in our vocabulary with the word 'will'.

So, instead of 'I CAN'T see myself owning a home one day', it will be 'I WILL own a home one day'. Instead of 'I CAN'T run my own business', it will be 'One day I WILL be a business owner'.

What you do just by changing your vocabulary is change your thinking, which in turn will change your actions. What you need to understand is that your words have a real effect on your actions. I am not for one second suggesting that things will become so much easier overnight and all of a sudden you will wake up with everything that you desire. What I am suggesting is that by changing the direction with which you approach your dreams, your goals and even the problems that are stopping your progress right now, you will, by a positive thought and action process, start seeing the small issues for what they really are. Small. Trust me, you will be faced with some monster problems along the path to success. That is when you need to have all of your focus. Don't waste it on the small and insignificant issues.

You can achieve anything you wish and you can overcome any obstacle. The choice is all yours.

Finding your faults 7

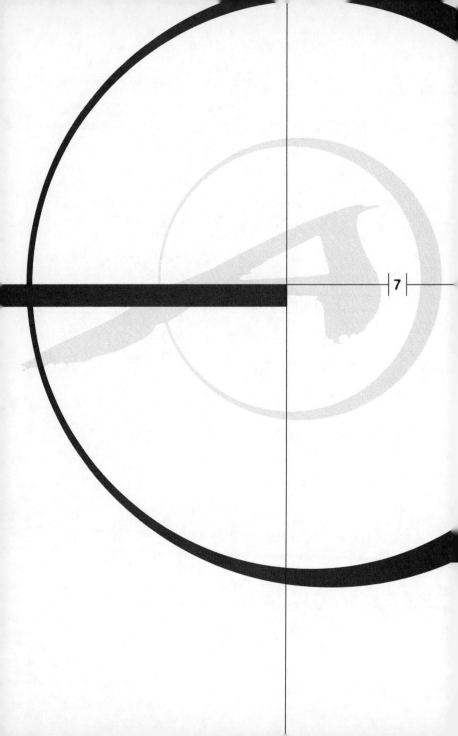

7

Among the first obstacles you will encounter along the route to achieving your dreams are your faults and failings. 'FAULTS!!!' I hear you scream. 'I don't have faults!!'

Well, let me tell you, you do—like it or not—and the fact that you can't admit it is probably your first and biggest fault! (If you are a male like me, you will definitely think you have no faults.)

Just because you have faults does not mean that you are any worse off than those around you. Everyone has his or her own faults. Some faults are very noticeable to everyone else, while others are hidden, out of sight—only you know that they are there. Regardless of how big or small, the fact remains that faults need to be addressed and overcome at some point in time. Why not start today?

It is all too easy to go through life without addressing any of the faults you have that will slow you down. We are very quick to point out someone else's faults and failings, but no-one dare do that to us or look out, we may chuck a hissy fit and get upset. Some of us even have the hide to think that we have it all together.

Instead of waiting for others to point out your faults, why not address them yourself and fix them once and for all?

Understanding your faults and weaknesses, I believe, is a major sign of strength. Not too many people, however, would willingly admit to those around them the areas in which they feel they are lacking. Today is the day to address those faults, no matter how big or small they are. That way you will release yourself into bigger and better things for your life.

You see, if you don't address your faults, what you are basically saying is that you are accepting the fact that you don't care if you don't grow—which in turn will be the exact excuse you will use when everything is not going how you thought it would. You know the one, 'Why didn't anyone tell me that I needed to address these areas?' Blaming others is one of the first signs that you have faults. Nor is it up to others to point out where you are going wrong. It is your life, your dreams and in the end your responsibility to address everything about who you are, good or bad.

There are two areas I want to cover in this chapter. The first is how we find those faults within ourselves, and how we handle them; the second is how do we handle others pointing out our faults, whether they are right or wrong?

First, let's look at you. Even better, *you* look at you. What faults do you know you have without having to even think about it? I can guarantee you could probably make a list of five to ten things straight away. That is a good thing. These are the faults that can be addressed and overcome fairly easily because they are always on the surface.

It is the other areas—you know the ones, the faults that people really close to you bring up right when you don't want to hear them—which you need to overcome the most. They are the things that we continually hide from ourselves, just hoping that they will either go away or never appear again.

If you are anything like me, you will believe that at most times you have everything together. You know that there are a few little niggling things that you could work on, but there isn't really much that you need to address. Your life and plans are all going the way you would like them to and nothing is going to stop your progress. But you are also very aware of the comments that occasionally come your way from those close to you highlighting an area or two that, as far as you are concerned, you have together, so that must mean that those close to you have no idea. You might think that what they are trying to do is pull you down because they don't want you to succeed. WRONG!!!

They might just want the best for you. It could be that you yourself are your worst enemy. Well, it is those little comments that are constantly repeated that we need to look out for. Just remember: if you don't find your faults, others around you will, and most times they will be quite blunt in pointing them out.

In most cases those loved ones around you have your best interests in mind. If you are constantly hearing certain faults being brought up, then maybe, just maybe, there is an area that needs adjusting. Which brings us to the second area— how we handle criticism.

Never let yourself get to the point where you think that you have outgrown advice and constructive criticism. This is one area that I have really had to work hard on. I hate being shown where I am lacking. I hate having those close to me point out where I am dropping the ball. But I love the feelings that I have (and they are lifelong feelings) when I address those areas and move on to bigger and better things.

Pride is a wonderful thing, but pride can and will slow you down and potentially move you away from your goals and dreams, purely because you have allowed it to get in the way.

Our opinions of ourselves may not always be a true gauge. We all need those close friends and family around us to give us third-party influences and opinions. Trust me, it may hurt sometimes, it may sting the old pride and hurt the ego, but it will also send a huge wake-up call which, if taken with the right attitude, can challenge you to get back on course.

Don't get too caught up in the whole fault-finding mission though. What I mean by that is that sometimes we can sit and stare forever into our navels trying to find the deepest and darkest faults, then try to dig deeper, and so on. All you need to do is find the fault, address it, fix it and then move on to living a better and fuller life. It is that simple. Don't over-complicate the process. All that will do is make you want to run away from the faults instead of towards fixing them.

Remember, though, that for some of you those faults have been ingrained as part of who you are for a long time. It has taken you years to be who you are, with those attitudes, those feelings and those reactions. That being the case, it may take a lot of effort to overcome them.

When it comes to addressing your faults, and mind you they may only be small ones, what you do need to do is to look at your life through a pair of 'honesty glasses'. You need to approach the whole process with a sense of honesty so that you are able to address the areas behind the surface faults that are obvious to you and everyone around you. If you don't address them properly, all you end up doing is fixing the surface, visible symptoms and leaving the root problem behind. You will then have to address the same issues again later as they were never dealt with properly in the first place. If your garden has weeds, they will continue to grow until you pull out the roots. Just removing what you can see will not solve the problem.

Being honest with yourself may be the hardest thing to do, but if done properly you will set yourself apart from those who continually cheat themselves by thinking that everything is taken care of. Have you ever looked at yourself and realised that new shirt or dress really doesn't look that good, but worn it anyway—then had someone blurt out what they really think of your outfit? Their honesty may offend you, but in reality you knew it all along. You may get all defensive, but what is the point when you know they are right? Things would have been a whole lot less painful if only you had listened to your own feelings about your outfit from the start.

It is the same with the faults that you know about right now. Why wait for someone else to bring them up if you can identify and address them by yourself? Why get yourself all worked up over someone's comments when you can avoid all that by fixing those issues yourself?

Let's use this fault-finding process in a business example. If you own a business then finding the faults in that business should be one of your highest priorities. You see, if your customers have to endure your faults just because you couldn't be bothered fixing them yourself, you will end up losing your customers. I was recently treated to an extreme example of this attitude.

My wife and I bought a spa for our backyard last year. This was something that we had long wanted, and had decided that now was the time. I looked around, went through various brochures and decided on a company that was a manufacturer as well as a retailer. This way I thought that not only would I get a good price, I would also get a good finished product. We picked out our spa, added the extra features we wanted and placed our order, arranging for the spa to be delivered before Christmas so we could enjoy it over our holidays.

It wasn't until the following February that we ended up receiving our spa. We had paid for delivery, but upon dispatch I was informed that I needed to have three extra people to help lift the spa at my end as 'delivery' only meant they would bring it to our driveway. (HUH? So much for the delivery service and cost.)

After only two days the problems started. First the waterproof stereo got water in it, which made it inoperable. I rang the company, only to be told that we must have done something wrong. The following day I went to use the spa with my daughter and found all the water had drained out because the pipes had been left undone. Once again I rang the company. The following day the control pad got water into it and, for the second time, we had to get the stereo replaced due to water damage.

All this time we were waiting for the spa cover to turn up, as the one that had been delivered was two sizes too small. Then the stereo had to be replaced *again* due to water damage and, to top it all off, the water drained out a second time.

I had had enough; I rang up to find out the name of the managing director. I was told his name and proceeded to write him a very long and detailed letter referring to the poor product and service that we had received and the treatment we were given throughout the entire ordeal.

What response did we get? NOTHING!

I rang again a week later only to be told that the person I had written the letter to was *not* the managing director. In fact, the managing director was the woman I had originally spoken to to get the managing director's name. Talk about unethical!

You could see from a mile away that there were some major issues within this company. The problem was the people involved could not see that there was anything wrong with what they were doing. I was castigated over the phone for complaining too much. The 'customer service' manager told me that the staff in the office now didn't want to talk to me when I rang up because they knew that there would be something that needed to be fixed. I was even told, 'Some of our customers don't even deserve our service, Mr Herald.' I was flabbergasted!

Here was a customer (me) pointing out the obvious, but as far as they were concerned they didn't have any faults—all the faults were the customer's. The customer seemed to just get in their way every day, which was a bit strange seeing they were in a business that relied on customers to grow! Any business that thinks they are better than their customers is doomed to fail. I would love to see if the company is still in business in a year's time with that type of attitude.

When you are approached by someone pointing out your faults, you have two options: you can listen to them and act upon those comments, or you can ignore them. Ultimately, the end result will depend on what you do with those comments.

Not everyone will be right when it comes to pointing out your faults—that is a fact. But the day that you close yourself off from letting those close to you influence your life for the better is the day that you will stop growing.

Be careful, though, about who you allow to influence your life. There will be many people who will point out what they say are your faults, when in reality all they want to do is bring you down. I only allow those close to me to point out the areas I need to address. I know they only want the best for me. You will find people around you who don't really care if you are offended by what they say. It is those people you need to avoid at all costs, as they can bring a destructive element into your life.

You can listen to those around you who are pointing out areas that you need to address, or you can choose to ignore their observations. That choice is entirely yours. Just remember, though, if you ignore everything that is said to you, pretty soon you will be left to deal with your faults on your own. Don't then throw the blame onto those around you. Blame is all too easy to give away. Don't give it away, keep it for yourself.

The truth is, all too often our faults are blatantly obvious to everyone around us but not to ourselves. Read the signs, watch what people are saying to you and address those issues. Even better, get in first—look at yourself and address the big and little faults that for years have been stopping you from achieving all that you can.

Once you address your faults, whether they are big ones or small ones, you will set yourself back on the path to achieving all that you desire for your life. The process of change will change your future. Now that's worth getting excited about! So, what are you waiting for!?

Aarghh!
The victim mentality

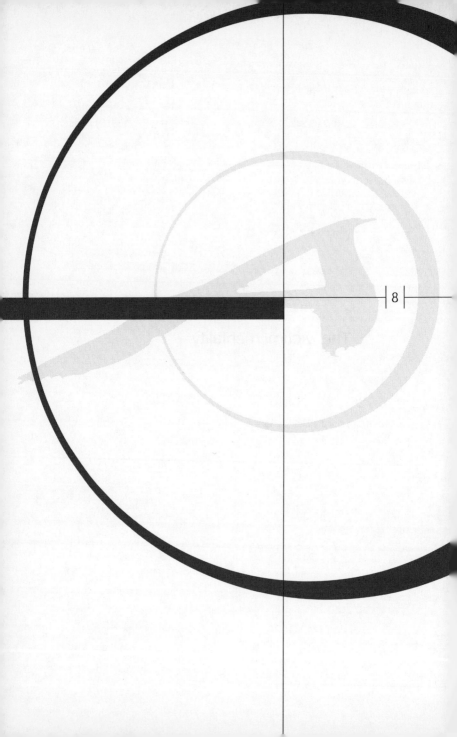

8

Those of you who have read my first book, heard me speak at a conference or seminar, or even spoken to me one on one, will understand my feelings about people who continually play the victim.

I can't stand the people who try to get ahead by manipulating everyone around them to feel sorry for them. They hope that by doing this, they will get others to accomplish what they want to achieve for them. It makes me so angry. Manipulating people's emotions is by no means something to be proud of. All these people are proving is that they have no desire to work at achieving anything through their own efforts, that they will use underhanded, low tactics to get ahead no matter who they use, and all too often hurt, in the process. Sooner or later they will find themselves distanced from others as a result, as no-one likes being emotionally used.

You will know who these people are. They are the ones who are constantly taking and never giving back. They are emotionally draining, wanting you to help them all the time but never taking your advice. Then when you are in need of a friend, or just someone to talk to, they are never around or they are always 'too busy'. But as soon as you achieve something, there they are, back again, like a leech trying to suck every bit of life out of you.

Selfishness is the tell-tale signature of the victim mentality. It is all about *them*. No matter whether their lives are going well or going a bit pear-shaped, victims will always turn things around to make themselves look as though they are at a disadvantage so everyone around them has to pander to their insecurities.

As I train at the gym most mornings, I have begun to notice certain patterns among some of the regulars. I don't like wasting time when I train; I like to stay as focused as I can, get the job done, do my various exercises and get to the office. The older I get the less time I like to spend doing physical activity, so I tend to spend as little time as possible talking to those around me when I am at the gym.

For some people, the gym seems to be a place where they can just talk all day, which to me defeats the purpose of even turning up. I see some people come in the door, stand around and talk for 30 minutes to an hour and then go home, all without raising a sweat. Recently I have been noticing a woman who goes about her gym session the same way every time she comes in. As she starts training, one of her friends will turn up and they'll get into a conversation straight away. She then proceeds to go through everything that she feels is wrong with her body shape that day and what she is unhappy about within her own life, until she hears the words 'I think you look great'. Then she will move on to train a little bit more—that is, until someone else she knows comes in. She will then go up to that person and discuss with them what she feels is wrong with her body that day until—yes, you guessed it—she hears the words 'I think you look great'.

She moves through most of the people she knows every time she is at the gym, operating the exact same way. All she wants to hear is what she wants to hear. She is playing the victim game where she wants others to build her up, but only in the way she feels fit. She is only interested in herself. I am yet to hear her ask or even comment on someone else.

All she is doing is fishing for what she thinks will make her feel better. She needs to start believing in herself instead of other people's comments. I don't feel that she would take it very well if someone told her that she needed to lose more weight, she needed to tone up a bit or she was whingeing too much.

I've also noticed that some weeks she talks to nearly everyone, then the next week cuts down her list because she didn't get the response she wanted from certain people the previous week. She will only listen to those who she knows will pander to her insecurity. Soon, I believe, she will run out of people to build her up as everyone will clue in to the fact that they are really only there to make her feel good.

Having a mentality that makes you out to be a victim is not the way to go. All you do by this is admit defeat by acting upon a negative platform. It is all about what you *think* you need to hear, not what is *needed* to be said. In effect, you are saying to yourself that you are giving up, that you will blame everyone else for everything bad that you have or will have to go through for the rest of your life. You believe that you are right and justified in your thinking and actions no matter what anyone else says.

Then there is what I call the handout mentality, a version of the victim mentality that basically says that everybody owes you. You may have put in the hard work over the years, you may have tried to get ahead, you may have even tasted success and lost it all, and now you believe that the world owes you.

No matter where you have been in your life, what you have been through or what unfortunate things may have happened, if you want to reach those goals and dreams you have set for yourself, you are the one that needs to get you there. By thinking that you are 'owed' you will only force yourself backwards—because you aren't owed anything in life. And if you go about thinking life owes you, what you are creating for yourself is an environment that says 'it is okay to fall short of my goals because someone else will pick me up and take me to them'. You are under the delusion that everything will work out for you because you are owed success.

I have had the opportunity a number of times to speak to groups of long-term unemployed people. The majority of these people want to change their circumstances—they are sick and tired of being in the situation that they are in. However, there is a minority in that group that believes they are owed everything. They believe it is their right to be looked after by the government (in fact, it is us that looks after them, through our taxes). These people get caught up in the thinking that it is everybody else's responsibility to get them out of their situation, so they just sit back and create an environment that they get mentally stuck in.

What a joke. Nobody owes you anything. The minute you start thinking like this, you set yourself up to fall short of your goals and dreams every time. The only person that owes you anything is the person reading this chapter right now. YOU!

The handout mentality of this minority needs to change from one of victim to one of victor over their own situations. Sure, they may have been dealt a rough hand with past employment, and sure they may have made some bad choices, but ultimately, their situations will only change when they do. What they need to do is walk away from the mentality that they are victims within their own lives and their own circumstances. That method of thinking is a destructive one. The problem with thinking like that is that you start to believe that you are forever at a disadvantage. As I have said many times already, the only way your situation will change tomorrow will be through the changes *you* implement within your thinking and in turn in your actions—today.

As soon as you take on the mindset of a victim, you will start to create a lifestyle that will create more of the same. You will approach everything that you work on, whether it is in your personal, family or work life, with a sense of victimisation. You will start to view everyone around you in a distorted way, especially if they are experiencing some success. You will see them as the enemy. Your jealousy will rule every thought and action. You will despise anyone who is successful.

The other week, after I finished speaking at a corporate function, a middle-aged man came up to me. The first words that came out of his mouth were, 'It's okay for you, you grew up in a nice home.' He was completely correct; I sure did grow up in a nice home. But I could have gone either way. I could have made a success out of myself or I could have blamed everyone for everything that I did.

If you are going to excuse your shortcomings by blaming your past, then your future will never change. You see, you want everyone around you to sympathise with where you are in your life. You want everyone to 'feel and share your pain'.

This is probably the biggest mistake that you can make. By wanting others to come down to your level, you will alienate yourself from those who really do care about you. You are forcing yourself to be on the outer, essentially feeding your own monster. What happens then is that you begin to feel even more victimised, because no-one 'understands what I am going through'. No-one will; in reality, no-one will want to. What they do want is the best for you, and if all you are doing is self-destructing, then you will force them away from you.

It is a shame that we allow these negative attitudes and actions to take over and rule our lives. It is such a selfish way to live, playing the victim. If only we focused all that energy that we put into feeling sorry for ourselves (being negative) and channelled it into positive actions, imagine the results we would get straight away.

When we operate from the level of the victim mentality, what we are saying to ourselves and those around us is that we are not going to change, that we are happy living below our own acceptable standards, that everyone else has to accommodate our insecurities. You want those around you to sympathise with what you are going through, and even when they do you will still constantly point out to everyone why you are unable to excel in your life.

As you can see, this is a silly way to approach life, but I bet you have already thought of people around you who operate in this manner—perhaps it's even you! If you do go about life this way, you need to dramatically change your approach. Until you do you will be stuck doing the same old thing the same old way with the same old outcomes.

What you get out of life is a direct reflection of the effort you put into it. If all your effort is directed towards showing others why you can't reach what you want to reach, then it is quite obvious what you will end up with.

This last section is devoted to those reading this chapter who either know, or have just figured out, that they have been playing the victim game. STOP!!! Understand that the longer you play the victim, the longer it will take you to achieve all that you want out of life. The only thing that you will gain from playing the victim is pain. You will end up losing those around you purely because you refused to change your outlook. No-one likes a whinger; no-one likes someone who blames everything except themselves for their outcomes.

Be victorious over your circumstances. Take control over your destiny. There will be people who will try to knock you down throughout your journey—just make sure one of those people isn't you. What's happened in the past is gone—it's in the past. All you need to concentrate on is what is going to happen to you in the future.

Change victim into victor. That is what you can control.

If nothing changes,
nothing changes!

9

I've talked at some length about the obstacles that stand in the way of change. Now I want to talk about change itself, and how to go about making changes.

Change is a word that many of us try to avoid. It may send a shiver down your spine. Some may even see it as a swear word. We don't want to hear it mentioned, we don't want to apply it, we just don't want anything to do with that word and what it represents. Maybe change is something you have tried in the past with little or no result, so you think that it will be better if you just go about your life the same way. That way you will avoid any dramas by not addressing them. WRONG! You may be thinking to yourself that this chapter is not really for you because you don't need to change any areas of your life. WRONG AGAIN! Every one of us needs to address change in one or more areas of our lives. No-one is excluded from this process.

By addressing change we will overcome a lot of the recurring issues and hurdles that we have faced in our lives—not only in business and work but also, and more importantly, in our personal lives. So why is it that many of us would prefer to stay the same, hanging on to those issues that in reality are stopping us from moving forward? Too many people try to go through their lives doing the same old things the same old ways. While this may feel comfortable, and even feel 'right', it will not bring you closer to your goals and dreams.

Let me explain. As the title of this chapter suggests, if we are not prepared to address the changes we need to make we will end up doing the same things the same ways, with the same results, so that what we end up with is frustration. It is we who create that situation, yet we still continue down the same path.

If you want to be different and better tomorrow then you have to address change in your life today. Some changes may only be small, others will be bigger. The biggest changes I have had to make in my life have been in the areas that are perhaps least visible and obvious to others; that is, my attitudes, my thought processes and even my relationships.

The first area I had to address when I started Attitude Inc.® was my attitude towards money, which really sucked. I never appreciated the value of money. That was why, at 25, I only had $50 to my name. I used to spend my money as soon as I got my pay cheque. I never looked at, or even thought about, the long term. I just wanted to live for the now and trusted that the tomorrows would look after themselves.

If I hadn't addressed that area at the very beginning of Attitude Inc.®, there is absolutely no way that I would be sitting here today living the dream that I am. Some of you may have no issues with money but others will understand exactly where I am coming from. I had to overcome that issue, and I mean *really* address it, before I could move on with anything else in my business life.

Don't hang on to the things in your life that have always been there just because you think they are part of what makes you you—especially if those things are the reasons you aren't reaching your full potential.

For some people, their issues and problems are a bit like a security blanket. They refuse to let go of them. Sometimes it seems easier to hang on to those issues so you can use them to excuse your shortcomings. They become a crutch to lean on as we excuse our failings to ourselves and anyone else who will listen.

Some people go through life with what I call the 'loser's limp'. Have you ever played a sport where you were winning and your opponent suddenly 'tripped', then started limping so the game had to be called off due to 'injury'? It doesn't just happen in sport. As soon as the going gets a bit tough, no matter what they are doing, some people develop a 'limp' that they expect everyone else to pander to; by doing this they think it will excuse their less-than-impressive results. They even end up convincing themselves that they are at a disadvantage.

I believe that change brings about release. You see, when you strip away the stuff that is in reality holding you back, it will release your mind and, in turn, your actions to try new things, live differently and view all the areas of your life with a new and better perspective. It is that release that we all need to be aiming for. Too many people look at the pain of change instead of at the productivity that change will bring. There is no better feeling than thinking on a new level or acting on things that you never thought you would. And all of this as a result of changing something about who you are or the way you go about life!

Change brings about a clarity that makes you see a better and clearer picture of your life. Clarity is one thing that seems to be missing in a lot of people's vision. Their goals and dreams are too blurry. Sure, they know that they have some goals and dreams, but they don't have the clarity of vision to know exactly where they actually are or what it will require to achieve any of those goals and dreams once they are set.

I am not sure about you, but after years of constantly falling short of my goals and dreams I was prepared to try reaching them in different ways to the methods I'd tried in the past. Up until I was 25, while I tried to achieve some of my goals, the whole time I was really staying the same, going about life trying to make everything fit around me and who I was back then. Not once did I clue in to the fact that it could be me and the way I approached and viewed my life that was the reason for not getting anywhere.

What have you been doing the same way for as long as you can remember? What do you want out of life but as yet failed to achieve? Who are you blaming instead of yourself? Maybe, just maybe, by changing your methods or approach, you will start to make more progress towards your goals.

Too many people prefer to stick to their comfort zones— they don't want to confront the issues and areas that are blocking their path. They would rather leave them alone, not disturb them, in the vain hope that they'll just disappear of their own accord. Well, this will not happen, and the longer you leave issues that need to be addressed, the longer it will take you to overcome them and move on and forward to all that you want out of life.

It is the same principle as mould. If you leave it on your shower wall for a year, the effort eventually required to remove it will be far greater than if you'd cleaned your shower every week. So constantly take a magnifying glass to your life and find those things that are stopping or slowing down your progress before it becomes too late.

Don't expect a different you the next day though. This is a big mistake a lot of people make. Then, due to the frustration of no immediate result, they go back to the same old them. It has taken many years to be who you are today. The way you view your life, the way you handle the issues in your life, even the way that you react, has been formed over many years. That being the case, you can't reasonably expect everything to change overnight just because you *want* it to. You need to work, and I mean really hard, on those issues until you force yourself to approach everything you do in a totally different way.

Remember, you only get a diamond out of a lump of coal after a huge amount of long-term pressure. You will need to endure that pressure to get the diamond out of your own life. If you give up too early, then you'll have to settle for the lesser result.

You have all probably heard the saying, 'if it ain't broke, don't fix it'. Well, I disagree with that, or at least I think it's a bit one-dimensional. We all need to take a good hard look at ourselves and our situations to see whether anything is broken, or even whether there might be some cracks appearing. How hard and deep do you look? Do you just address issues as they arise? Or do you keep your eye out for cracks starting to appear? The same cracks that if left alone may turn into life-altering dramas.

Too many people wait until the big cracks appear before they start addressing them. In one way big cracks are easier to repair than small ones because they are more obvious. However, there can be many tiny cracks in our lives that have the potential to expand into big cracks all at the same time if we are not careful.

I have had a large number of broken bones during my life, most of them as a result of being young and stupid. I have had a few hairline fractures as well. Most of the hairline fractures could not be easily found as they were tiny. There was a lot of pain, but if I had not gone and had an X-ray and started treatment, eventually the problem that started off as a little crack would have developed into a major break, leaving me in even more pain and with potentially worse problems down the track.

That is the way some of us address problems in our lives. For the things that stand out and are obvious to both ourselves and those around us, we change. But it is the little things that, if left unchecked and unchallenged, will go from small issues, or hairline fractures, to major problems that will cause us to slow down and maybe even alter our direction. It may ultimately take much longer to get back on track. What a waste of time, all because we were unwilling to look a little bit more closely and with an open mind about what needed changing.

You see, it is sometimes in areas that you don't normally consider where major turnarounds will occur in your life. A lot of people won't consider change because they are comfortable the way they are right now and if they upset the applecart it may tip over. They understand there are areas that may need a little attention, but because they feel that it will open up too many issues they just leave well enough alone.

It is easy to see why many of us feel like this but the reality is the opposite. With change, and I mean well-thought-out, planned change, comes a sense of release and purpose. I'll explain. Imagine that you have been trying to achieve your dreams for many years. While you have had some successes you still are largely falling short of your desired outcomes and frustration is starting to set in, which is leading you to make silly decisions and half-hearted commitments.

By changing your outlook, your approach and maybe even your methods, you open up a whole new outlook. You start to see that by doing things the way you were before, you were constantly playing catch-up instead of putting your entire effort into achieving those dreams. The view is a lot different when the clutter is taken out of the way. You may even find that your dreams and goals are closer than you thought.

Living a full and prosperous life requires effort. It isn't easy. That being the case, you don't need the added pressure from issues that are repeatedly popping their collective heads up and keeping you from your goals. Your attention should be focused on the bigger picture, not the areas that are keeping you from all that you desire.

With an unblocked focus you are able to reach your goals a

lot quicker. If you are battling the same problems (no matter how big or small) all the time, it is plainly obvious that achieving success is going to take longer. What we all need to do is overcome the areas that are slowing us down, move on and direct our attention towards our goals and dreams instead of those areas that are giving us nothing but negative outcomes.

To recap what I said in Chapter 3, probably the biggest factor behind people failing to reach their goals and live the life they want is that they were unsure about what they wanted in the first place. This may sound like a stupid comment, but let me explain. Many people go through life waiting for something good to 'happen', without really knowing what it is they're waiting for. We all need to ask ourselves what it is we actually want out of our lives. Without direction we will go nowhere.

People who complain about being nowhere near where they wanted to be at this time in their lives might never have set out for themselves a plan or path to follow. They might have tried to follow someone else's path—this never works—or they might have given up before they started because they thought they had too many issues to address. We all need to make plans, we all have issues and we all constantly need to make changes in our lives.

Don't think for one minute that once you have addressed your issues that you will be fine for the rest of your life, however. We all need to address the area of change every day. The minute you stop is the minute your journey will plateau. Trust me, the areas I need to address today are way bigger and harder to address than those I faced when I first started my business. With success comes responsibility. Not only to others but also, more importantly, to ourselves. We need to be responsible to ourselves first. That way we will be able to help others along the way from a perspective of personal understanding, not just fancy rhetoric.

Figure out today what you want and where you want to go. Once you have done that, you can then address the areas that will require change and attention. Don't just 'go with the flow', as all this does is put you under the control of situations and circumstances around you. Take charge, be in control and start changing the areas today that are slowing you down.

No sacrifice equals
no reward

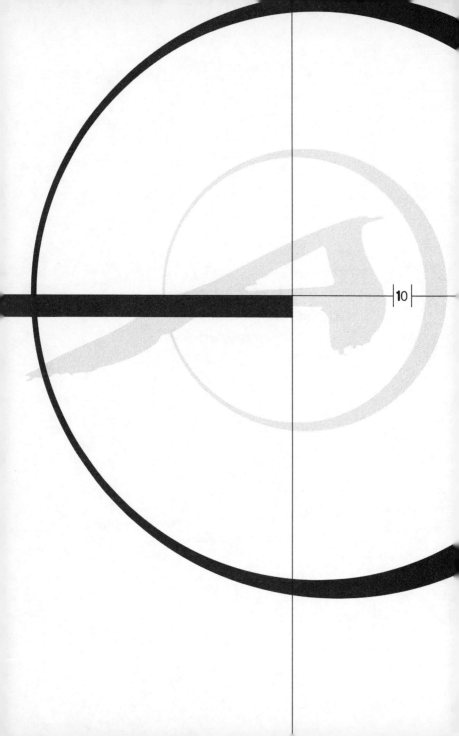

|10|

The word 'sacrifice' seems to scare people half to death. When they think of sacrifice, they automatically think of what they are losing instead of what they may be gaining. In this chapter I want to change your view of this word and this process. I talked in my first book about 'spring-cleaning', a process that I undertake every three months where I look hard at those around me and even harder at myself. I look at my business associates, my friends and even the people I have irregular contact with. If any of those people are making me take my eyes off what I am trying to achieve, or if I am having a negative effect on them, then I spring-clean them out of my life. I never do it in a way that would hurt them, or in a way that makes me out to be better than they are, I just disassociate from them, slowly and gradually.

The reason behind this is that sometimes, while I may enjoy the company that some of these people provide, I am also very conscious that I am needing to better myself every day and to do that I need to move forward every day. If I have the same people with the same issues around me all the time, then really I am going about my life the same every day.

Recently I bought my wife a new car. Vanessa's last car was a four-wheel-drive that couldn't fit into our two-car garage, so she parked it outside every night. The new car was her pride and joy, it would fit in the garage and she wanted to have it locked away every night.

The problem was that our garage was a mess. You will probably understand what I am talking about. We had stuff everywhere. We had things that had been systematically moved from inside the house over the years, even things that Vanessa and our daughter Jade had bought at garage sales—other people's junk that had become our junk. I mean we had stuff everywhere. The solution to the problem was pretty simple. We had to clean up the garage so there was room for Vanessa's new car. A fairly simple task, you would think—but no!

There were things of mine, things of Vanessa's and all of Jade's old stuff that we had hung on to for years and just didn't want to let go of. One Saturday we decided that this was the big 'clean up the garage day'. We started by pulling out everything that blocked Vanessa's car space and put it on the lawn to go through later. Then we thought that while we were at it we would clean up the rest of the garage as well.

We put my stuff in my pile, Vanessa's stuff in her pile and Jade's stuff in her pile. That way we could each go through our own piles and throw out or give away what wasn't needed any more. There was one rule. Be ruthless.

Well, I must say I learnt something about myself that day. I am a hoarder. When I came to sort through my pile, everything in it was so important to me that I didn't want to get rid of anything! There were things in that pile that I didn't even know I had or hadn't needed or used for months—even years—but I wanted to keep it all, 'just in case' I needed it one day. When we'd all gone through our piles, mine seemed to be the same size as when I started. I just couldn't grasp the concept of being ruthless that day. In the end Vanessa came to my rescue and whittled my huge pile of useless garbage down to just a few small things.

This is the same sort of thing that happens every day in everyone's life. We hang on to so much stuff without even thinking about it, not realising that we really don't need it. I am not talking about physical stuff; I am talking about emotional stuff, attitudinal stuff and even old relationship stuff. We are afraid that if we let go of this extra baggage we will be left an empty shell.

What we all need to do is get rid of this stuff so that we can park our 'new car' or, in real terms, our 'new you' in its place. By clearing the garbage out of our lives we will make more room for the good things we need to put around us to make us better people, better friends and maybe even better workers. The garbage that we hang on to stops us from pressing forward. It acts as a wall to our thinking and in turn our actions.

Some of the things you need to spring-clean from your life may be part of what you think makes you you. We all at some point in our lives (some of us every day) try to use this notion as an excuse for our faults. Your attitude towards this whole chapter might give you an insight as to where you need to start working. You might be thinking that none of it applies to where you are right now, because you have got it all together. You might *think* that you have spring-cleaned all the old junk in your life that was holding you back. But have you?

I don't believe that we ever clean everything out once and for all. Every day we allow junk to filter into our thinking and our actions. We get offended by what people say, we take falling short of achieving something to heart, we may even allow our insecurities to creep back in some days.

You see, no matter how far we've travelled on our way, we still need to address issues and feelings every day. If we don't, and we just cruise along through life without looking at ourselves and the progress of our journey, we will get a big surprise when we find we are way off course.

I am not one to be told what my faults are. I hate it. I get my back up and my nose out of joint. It wasn't until I realised how many people were commenting on certain issues (or, for a better word, faults) that I started to question whether I was the one who still had things that needed to be worked out. This is an area that we all need to address.

While we may have an idea of where we are lacking and what we need to work on, those who are close to us will have a more objective picture of who we are. As long as it is done in a nice and gentle way, your close friends and family will have the ability to help you master some of these areas. If it is done in a mean-spirited and vindictive way, however (as can happen), the best way to handle that situation is by not reacting or retaliating. I know what you are thinking—'easier said than done'. You are right. But why waste your time and energy proving others wrong just to make yourself look right?

It's funny, you know. When you reach a level of success in your life, all of a sudden you start to convince yourself that you have overcome all of the issues you had and you forget (on purpose sometimes) that you still need to make sacrifices.

You've probably all made a list of the goals you want to achieve, but did you also list the things you'll need to sacrifice to get you to those goals? This is a very important part of goal-setting. Without thinking about what it is going to take, what you are doing is setting yourself up for surprises. Surprises are things that you should avoid at all costs if you can help it. Why wait for issues to pop up and surprise you if you have the chance to address them first? By doing this you will definitely save yourself some pain, not to mention the time better spent addressing issues that could have been dealt with at the start of your journey.

As Jade is in her last year of primary school at the time of writing this book, her school workload and homework have increased. She is being prepared for the extra work that will be required when she starts high school. Jade is very similar to both Vanessa and me when it comes to her homework. She hates it. She sometimes thinks that we take great pleasure in making her sit and do her homework every day as well as her studies. (Man, I seemed to have turned out just like my parents!)

Now I would love for Jade to be outside playing and spending time with her girlfriends, but she needs to understand the principle of sacrifice for herself. If she didn't sacrifice her time for her studies, there is a high possibility that she would struggle to understand what she is being taught and not get the most out of her education—which might put her at a disadvantage at a later date. Her reward for her sacrifices will eventually be a great outlook for her future.

Sometimes the rewards for our sacrifices may not be evident straight away. It may take a long time for those rewards to shine through. Many of us focus on what we are losing, all that we have to sacrifice, when what we should be looking at is what we are gaining in the long run. It is a different view, but it is a positive view instead of a negative one. If all you ever focus on are those things that you may lose, then I can guarantee you will never make the sacrifices you need to make.

Achieving our dreams is all about looking further than the present. Sure, in reality we will be giving some things up, maybe even things that we think make us who we are. But the reality is that if we want to grow into better people, to reach those goals and dreams that we have planned for ourselves, then we need to make radical changes in our thought processes and actions.

Your dreams and goals will not happen by themselves. There is one important ingredient, and without it they will never eventuate. That ingredient is YOU! Now that you know this, what type of you are you willing to be to reach those goals you have set yourself? A 'just get by' you, or an 'excellent' you?

The story of me starting with only $50 and turning it into a worldwide licensing brand has been widely publicised. What the reports rarely go into are the sacrifices I had to make, such as the part-time jobs I had just to keep myself afloat. When first starting Attitude Inc.® I had the biggest plans, goals and dreams anyone could have. It was great to have those goals, but I had to sell my first shirt to be on my way. I had to do the small stuff before I could handle the big dreams.

I am the first to admit that the idea of working was not one that I really enjoyed. But the day that I started my business I had to change that mentality. I had to consciously decide that I was going to put in 100 per cent, no ifs or buts.

This sounds great now, but the rubber really hit the road when I started that first week. I realised straight away that my great business idea was in no way going to sustain me financially. I had to find another job so I could get Attitude Inc.® off the ground. I have to say I really questioned whether owning my own business was a smart choice that day. I had to decide there and then that I needed to make sacrifices. One of the biggest sacrifices was my time—my free time.

I am so glad I followed through with my goal. Sure I made sacrifices, and sure I didn't get to do what my friends were doing sometimes. But today I am able to look back without a regret and know that I made the right choices, the right sacrifices.

There is one more thing that needs to be pointed out when it comes to sacrifice. Sacrifice will affect your direction:

- Big sacrifices = big direction changes, resulting in BIG RESULTS.
- No sacrifice = no direction change, resulting in the same or NO RESULT.

Let me explain. In order to achieve your goals and dreams you are going to have to make some changes in your approach and make some sacrifices. For some they may be small sacrifices, for others they may be large. Remember, though, if you concentrate your focus and your attention on what you have to give up and sacrifice, you will only end up looking backwards at what you gave up instead of forwards to your goals and dreams. Keep your eyes firmly focused on what is ahead.

You are not alone. We all need to address sacrifice at some time, if not many times, in our lives. The difference between those who are successful and those who are not is the degree of sacrifice they have made.

Stickability

Stickability is one of the major factors that people overlook when trying to reach their own goals and dreams. (You won't find this word in a dictionary as it's made up.) Sticking to what we started all those years ago is essential to achieving the desired outcome. I know that some of you may be saying to yourselves, 'I know that!' Well then, why are there so many people today who are now realising that they need to get back on track?

I don't for a minute claim to be teaching you anything new. As they say, you can't reinvent the wheel, but what I am endeavouring to do is to make the wheel roll a bit better, by explaining things in a way that will make a bit more practical sense.

Remember I talked earlier about understanding what you want out of life and setting your goals? Well, if you feel you have gone off track, which of your goals or dreams have you let go? What would you have been able to achieve if only you'd stuck it out through the tough times?

We are all guilty at some time or another of changing our mind and even our direction to take a different and less challenging path, one that is easier to handle. We have failed to stick to our original plans and goals. That is fine if we just want to get by in life, but if you are like me you should want to fulfil those dreams that you have had for a long time and open yourself up to a new part of your life.

It is easy to stick to your direction and path when things are going well, when everything seems to be going in a direction that you are happy with. You are on cloud nine. You know, the times when no matter what you do it all seems to turn to gold. You can't seem to do anything wrong. There is nothing wrong with that; in fact, that is what we all need to get to.

Those are the times when we all think we are bulletproof. Then reality hits and something goes a bit left of centre. Then it's panic stations, we start to overreact, and get way off the path we were heading along. Then we may want to give up as we think that this is the best course of action.

You see, it is through the hard times, through the periods when things just aren't working for us, that we learn more about ourselves than we do in the good times. It is our 'stickability', or commitment, in those hard times that will get us to our goals. If we can see past the problems that are staring us in the face and push through those barriers, we will open ourselves up to new and exciting challenges that will takes us to where we want to go, and potentially even further.

I believe that it is the tough times, the times when things need a lot of work and effort, that shape us for life. If you give up too early and don't stick things out, you will instil in yourself a defeatist mentality—one that will shape your future actions and reactions in a negative way. Let me give you an example that many of you may relate to.

After growing up in a loving home, watching my two parents love each other and display a 'perfect' marriage, I always thought that was how all marriages (especially mine) would be. Man, was I in for a shock. This thing they call marriage needs constant work.

We should all come with a manual letting our partners know what our strengths and, especially, what our weaknesses are. When you have problems or issues with each other they need to be worked out or else bigger problems and cracks appear. Now the easiest way to deal with these problems is to just quit, walk away and avoid any of the dramas. It is a fact that sticking it out and working out the problems makes for a stronger relationship and stronger marriage. If and when Vanessa and I have issues, they are mainly small (remember the hairline cracks?). They are about stupid little things that could get blown way out of proportion if we didn't deal with them. But we made a conscious agreement early on that we were not going to be another statistic.

The same theory applies to every other part of your life. You need to have a NO EXIT clause. By that I mean you need to determine that no matter what comes your way, what results you end up with, you will not take the easy way out and quit. You need to stick to your original plan—your original goals and dreams. By doing that it will force you to get results. The problem with quitting all the time is that you create a pattern of defeat, and once you create that pattern it is difficult to get out of it. It can shape your path in the future unless addressed.

A lot of us, myself included until I reached 25, create our own patterns of falling short of everything we are trying to achieve. We get used to failing and falling short, so that what happens is that we program ourselves for failure every time we try to achieve something. Straight away we are expecting to fail before we even start. It is no wonder that we go through life accepting second best when we have planned for it without even realising it.

Many people who experience some aspect of failing to reach a goal end up with what I call 'lowering disease'. Lowering disease is when you lower your expectations every time you set out to achieve something. While you may begin with high expectations, you start to lower the desired outcome before you even finish the planning process because, in your head, you have admitted to yourself that you cannot reach those 'ridiculous' goals. You have pre-programmed your thinking, which in turn affects your actions.

By lowering your focus you are limiting your vision. I am unsure about you, but I am sick and tired of being limited. Limits constrict your progress. I want to have no limits.

I was driving the other day to pick up my daughter from school. As I turned into the street her school is in, the sun was right in my eyes. The glare was so bad that I had to lower the sun visor of my car and slow right down. If your vision is blocked or hindered, your progress will slow down. That is a fact. What you need to do is make sure you are in total control of where your vision is. Is it blocked or is it clear? Do you just slow down or do you stop completely?

Imagine going to an archery field. You have all the best equipment, you line up your arrow, take aim, take the strain of the bow and, just as you are about to let the arrow fly, you change your mind because you think you might miss. You second-guess your aim. So instead of aiming for the target you shoot the arrow into the air. You think that you have accomplished something but what you have done is only half of the job. Sure you have shot an arrow, but you have failed to hit anything. Your negative thinking has affected your actions to a point where you even think that you have done something worthwhile when in fact you have just wasted your energy. The more effective approach would be to continually aim at that target until you hit it. Once you have hit it, you stick at it until you start hitting the bullseye.

While some people believe that success is easy, I can guarantee you that it isn't. I challenge you to talk to successful people around you and see if they became successful overnight. I bet that it took a lot of time and a lot of disappointments until they hit the target board. Then and only then did they hone their skills to start hitting their own bullseyes.

Another big mistake many people make is trying to hit too many targets with the one arrow. What I mean by that is that they start on their journey towards their goals and dreams and all of a sudden they want to start moving towards another goal that they have, then another. After a while they have so many goals in the pipeline that they start to take short-cuts. Soon they become frustrated because nothing is getting completed. This is a big issue that I am constantly coming across when people come up to me after I speak at functions. Due to their desire to achieve too much at once they get caught up in the doing and the busyness of the working instead of focusing on the achieving. The end result is that all they are dealing with is disappointment and resentment rather than the reward of reaching the goals that months, sometimes years earlier they had set for themselves.

Let me explain it a different way. Imagine I told you to stand 10 metres away from me. I then gently throw a ball for you to catch. Pretty easy, hey? What would happen if I throw the first ball to you, quickly followed by a second one. Still manageable? Probably. What if I now throw ten balls to you at the same time? How many do you think you would catch? One, maybe two.

This is the way many people approach their goals and dreams. They start with one goal and when they have some success they take on another mission. Then for some reason they start to try to accomplish all their goals at the same time. No wonder they end up with a whole lot of frustration and unfulfilled dreams.

The last element of stickability is using frustration as a motivator. I believe that we need to use frustration as a tool to get to where we want to be in our lives. Too many times when we get frustrated we read it as a sign that we are heading in the wrong direction.

I was totally frustrated in the first year of my business. I was frustrated at the lack of working capital, at the amount of negativity coming from people around me, at the fact that

I wasn't able to make and sell the products that I really wanted to. I could have interpreted that frustration as a sign that I just wasn't meant to be in the clothing business. But I am so glad I used it as a source of fuel to push myself on to bigger and better things. I was determined to stick to what I'd started no matter how frustrated I became. It is just another barrier or wall that we need to push through.

Don't be fooled. Frustration will change your course if you let it. What we need to do is turn that feeling of frustration into a fuel that drives us on to bigger and better things. It is what we focus on that will determine what we achieve. If there are too many things to focus on we will inevitably end up focusing on nothing but the blur of everything coming at us from all directions. If what you focus on is the frustration of not being able to achieve, then that is all you will see.

What we all need to do is stick to one goal at a time until we reach and fulfil it. By doing that we will create a positive habit. Then, based upon success, not frustration, we can move forward with a sense of accomplishment towards the next goal we have set ourselves. Remember, it is what you stick at that will be what you live.

Perseverance | 12 |

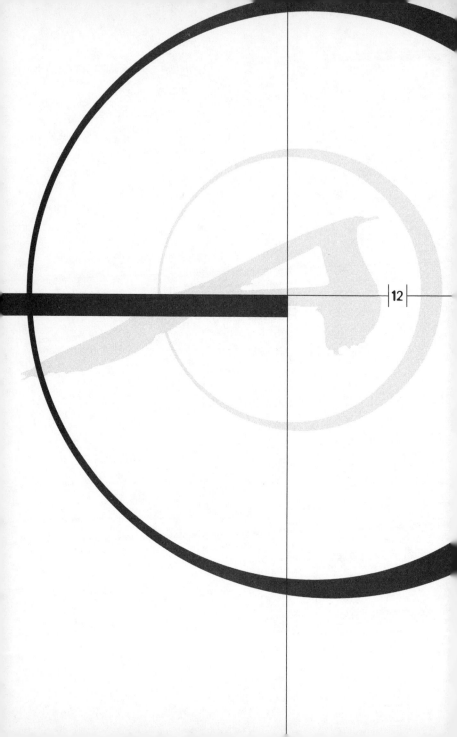

12

Along your journey towards reaching your goals, you will probably come to a time when you just want to give up. It is not that you aren't making any ground; it is that it just doesn't seem to be happening quickly enough for you.

I know exactly how you feel. When I first started Attitude Inc.® I knew exactly what I wanted to achieve, and yes, things did happen quite quickly (as some keep pointing out), but the problem I had to overcome was that I was wanting everything to happen even faster; as far as I was concerned it wasn't quick enough.

Please understand, though, that sometimes the frustration caused by impatience can ruin our resolve—we can head off in the wrong direction or just give up. If only we'd just persevered along the path we were heading, who knows where we would have ended up. Impatience is a terrible thing. Trust me, I know. I would have to be the world's most impatient person.

Perseverance means 'to maintain an effort'. Think about it. To persevere you need to maintain the same effort that you were inputting in the first place. This point is a very valid one. Many people think that perseverance is all about extra effort, when in reality it means that the same continuous effort is required, but for a longer period of time. A lot of people let their effort fade off after a while. They still think they are persevering towards their goals, and sure, they are still heading in the right direction. But their lowered effort level is the factor that in the end will be the thing that stopped their progress.

My daughter Jade is an absolute freak (in the nice way) when it comes to participating in any type of sport at school. Whatever is on she wants to go in it. Sometimes she will make up her own sport or game so she can conquer that as well. The thing about Jade that teaches me a lesson, every time she participates in anything, is that she will never give up until she has finished the task—no matter whether she comes first or dead last. Jade sees that finishing something is just as important as starting it. This is a quality that I know will serve her well throughout her life.

Recently Jade enrolled at a new school. She came home one day with a note about an upcoming cross-country race. This one race would determine the top three students in each age group who would represent the school at the state finals. On top of that, any laps after the set distance was completed would be classified as a fun run to raise money for the school through sponsorship organised by the students.

I have to say neither Vanessa nor I were overly confident that Jade would even finish the 4-kilometre distance, let alone raise any money out of extra laps, as this was the longest distance she had ever run at one time.

Jade went up the street, rang our friends and talked to our families, all the time raising the sponsorship money. She chose to collect the money up front before even starting the race. At the time I wasn't sure that this was the best idea, but Jade assured me she knew what she was doing.

The day came, and I have to say Jade was pumped. She was ready to go. She was up early preparing herself for the big day. She was running up and down our street getting warmed up. Jade (like her father) loves an audience, so Vanessa decided she would go and cheer her on.

Bang! The starter's gun went off and so did Jade. The field of runners all went out hard, some only making it through the first lap, but Jade kept pressing on. After many many laps Jade crossed the line in second position in her age group in the girls, and in front of many of the boys her age. She was into the state final. Did she get excited straightaway and rest? NOPE. She continued on without missing a step.

After a while Vanessa saw Jade starting to slow down. She was getting tired. Vanessa began to cheer her on. And I mean loudly. So much so, one of the teachers asked Vanessa if she would like to run alongside Jade to encourage her. (I personally think it was more like the teachers were over this screaming mother standing next to them.) Anyway, as Vanessa started to come alongside, Jade's pace picked up—she could sense her goal becoming a reality. Jade now had someone to share her pain and victory with.

Jade completed an extra 10 laps, the number she needed to complete for the money she had already collected. It was Jade's perseverance and persistence that got her to the finish line. She had to maintain that effort to live up to the expectations that she had placed upon herself. She had a goal that she wanted to reach regardless of the pain that was involved.

What is it that you have been trying to achieve for months, maybe even years? Are you maintaining the effort needed or have you let that effort level slip? If you have let it slip, then that is why you are falling short. Sure, there may be other factors that have contributed, but it is up to you to get things back on track.

Jade had Vanessa beside her to encourage her and share her pain. Who do you have beside you who will take on your journey and its experiences and pain? We all need people around us who can lift us up when we are down or struggling. Don't think for one minute that you don't. It is those around us, who are there to share our pain and frustrations, who will share our joy when we make it to our goals and dreams. You should never expect them to do your work for you, but to have someone to lean on is extremely important.

As Jade had collected the money before she started the race, she had pre-set her goal. Once she was at the starting line, straight away she knew what was required to achieve that goal; reality would have set in. She had to finish all the laps needed to raise the money. It was her perseverance that got her over the line. No matter how tired and sore she felt, she knew what she had to do. For Jade there was no giving up. That was not an option as far as she was concerned.

If you have pre-set goals, are you willing to do whatever it takes to get there? Are you willing to maintain the effort needed? Too many times we are guilty of giving up before we see the finish line. All we want are the rewards without the pain. It is the pain we experience that should act as our guide as to whether we are on the right track or not. Remember that old saying 'no pain, no gain'?

At the time of writing this chapter a man who had heard me speak rang me, basically to say that he thought that I had had it too easy and my progress was not relatable to his own situation, and that I had no right to share my experiences with anyone. I have to say that many thoughts crossed my mind as he was saying this but, ultimately, the reality was that he wasn't there with me every day over the seven years of my business, he didn't work the extra part-time jobs for the first few years. He was merely looking at the end result and trying to justify his own lack of effort and accomplishment. Trying to find fault in others is no way to bring you any closer to your dreams.

I am still wondering why someone would ring just to say what he said, but really, it is his own lack of perseverance and persistence that has got him to where he is. Don't play the blame game. I could probably sit here all day thinking of who did what to me over the years, but all that would do is excuse myself (in my head) for what I didn't achieve. Perseverance is what got me to where I am today, not luck and definitely not the easy road. But just like you, I don't have to excuse my success purely because others get offended by it.

I remember at the Sydney Olympics in 2000 a swimming race that captivated the world. It will not go down in history as the fastest race. It probably won't even be remembered as a must-see event in ten years or so. But it will be remembered by everyone who saw it as an absolute inspiration.

Eric Moussambani may not be a name that you recognise immediately, but if I said 'Eric the Eel' it will probably ring a bell. Eric the Eel was from Equatorial Guinea. He had come to the Sydney Olympics to race in the 100-metre freestyle. In his heat there were only two other competitors, who were both disqualified for jumping the starter's gun. This meant that Eric was to race in the pool by himself. Not much motivation there really. If it was you or me, we might just have given the race a miss.

The starter's gun went off and so did Eric. Slowly, very slowly. It was the slowest Olympic time ever recorded for the 100 metres, about a minute more than for the competitors who had raced earlier. He slowly swam up and down, all the while cheered on by the massive audience, which got louder and louder with every stroke.

Did he win a medal? No. Did he achieve anything? Absolutely. Eric the Eel showed everyone that no matter what obstacles lie in your path (not being able to swim being one), he believed in Sir Winston Churchill's advice to NEVER GIVE UP. At the halfway point he could have just thrown in the towel. He would have known that he was nowhere near the time needed to qualify for the next round. But he persevered until he reached the finish point.

It may take you much more time than you originally anticipated to reach those goals you have set for yourself, but until you start you will never know where the finish line is. To persevere, you need to have a belief in what you are trying to achieve. So often I am approached by people who want to achieve one or more of their goals but don't actually think they will make it.

With that type of mentality they probably never will. The biggest area they first need to understand is the concept of perseverance. If reaching your goals and living your dreams were easy, then everybody on this planet would be doing it. I know that I keep pushing this fact, but I really want it to sink into your thinking. It isn't easy and it does take time. It all comes down to whether you are willing to invest that time.

Let's break your journey into two sections:

1. The start.
2. The finish.

That is all there is. This may sound way too simple, but just bear with me. A lot of times all people look at is the finishing half. They have set their expectations on the finish line before they have lifted one muscle towards the starting blocks. It is the starting process that I believe is the most important— because if you don't start something, it will be absolutely impossible to finish it.

Imagine sitting in a room. On the other side of that room is a door that you need to walk out of (very similar to getting the cup of coffee I'd left in the kitchen that I referred to in an earlier chapter). Now you can stare at that door as long and as hard as you like, but until you make a step towards that door it will not get any closer. It is those steps, however many it takes, that will result in you reaching the door. You see, the door isn't really the prize. It is the steps that it takes to get there that will ultimately fulfil your desire to reach it. It is in those steps that you will learn the greatest lessons about yourself.

You see, for many, all they want is what is at the end of the effort. They don't see the effort required as having any value, they see it as a hindrance. BUT—it is in taking those steps towards that door that you will discover the keys to unlocking your goals and dreams.

Then there is the finish. Further to my example with my daughter Jade, if she had gone out as fast as she could, right from the starter's gun, she would have run out of energy and failed to finish. What she did was pace herself, and once the goal was in sight she then was able to run harder and faster because she hadn't worn herself out at the start.

What steps are you taking today to reach your goals? What have you stopped persevering with that if only you re-addressed would get you back on your path?

A marathon is a long race, but then again, so is reaching your goals. Persevere. Be determined to reach all that you want to reach no matter how hard or how long it takes. So, what are you waiting for?

Be a control freak

13

I am an absolute control freak by anyone's standards. Not that I try to take control over every situation, it is just that I would prefer to be the one who is in control, as that's the way I'm wired.

Earlier in my life I was out of control with no real direction, just doing whatever felt right at the time with no positive outcome, so now I make sure I control my outcomes. Not that every outcome is what I first planned, but at least I have some sense of control over the ending. You see, it is when you lose control over where you want to end up in life that things will start to fall apart. Then you make rash decisions without thinking of the outcome, which result in you heading off in the wrong direction and chasing your tail.

I hate being a passenger in a car and above all I hate being a passenger in a plane. All who know me well will attest to this fact. I have never had a bad flying experience, it is just a fear that I have. This is proving to be a bit of a problem lately, as many of my speaking engagements are interstate so it is basically impossible to avoid getting on a plane. Even so, I will try and think of any way possible other than flying to get me to my destination.

What I have put it down to is that I am not in control of flying the plane. Even if I was given the option one day to fly myself to the destination I am heading to, it wouldn't really help, as I have no idea how to fly! I have to put my trust in those who have trained for all those years to do their job and fly the plane.

But when it comes to my own life I have to take the driver's (or pilot's) seat. Unlike the plane, I do know how to control the outcomes that I desire. I have always had the attitude when it comes to my own goals and dreams that it is me who is the one that controls my direction and path. Sure, others will try and take over that control, but only if I allow them to do so.

My speaking engagements have virtually become a weekly occurrence and I am constantly in front of many people. As I am my own biggest critic, of everything that I do, I am always trying to better myself with the way that I deliver my speeches.

A few weeks ago I had the opportunity to speak to a crowd of over 1000 business owners at a public seminar put on by a magazine that I write for. At the end of my presentation I was in the foyer signing copies of my first book. I was nearly finished when a woman approached me and proceeded to tell me that she had some advice for me if I ever wanted to be a good speaker. She was just starting a new business in coaching speakers worldwide on how to communicate better.

Now, I must say, it probably wasn't the best time to come and pick my presentation to pieces straight after I had spoken, especially with around 50 people standing nearby. I asked her what it was that she thought wasn't any good. She told me that I walked around the stage too much and I put my hands in my pockets every now and then. I then asked her how often she had spoken in public. Never, was her answer.

Undaunted, however, she went on to tell me that without her services, my speaking career wouldn't last. I have to say I didn't see eye to eye with her, nor did any of the other people standing around waiting to talk to me.

Please don't think that I believe that I am perfect at public speaking. But I do know that the effect I have on people's situations when they listen to what I have to say is proof enough for me that what I do works.

You see, all she was doing was trying to control my method; she wasn't listening to my message. Sure I may walk around the stage, and sure, because I have nothing to do with my hands they may end up in my pockets. But I have realised that the only ones who criticise what I am doing with my speaking these days are the 'experts'. The audience seems to love what they see and hear. They understand that I am there to push them further on in their journey.

I want to be better at everything that I do, but I like to be the one in control of how that happens. The minute you allow others to come uninvited into your environment, you are allowing them to shape and change the outcomes. If you let others dictate your outcomes then you cannot complain about the end results.

As I do want to be better every day, I am the one who takes control over excelling myself. I don't want, or need, someone who is yet to achieve anything telling me how it should be done. This may sound harsh, but just ask yourself one question. How many times have you been given 'advice' from someone who has not even completed as much as you have in that situation? It's annoying, isn't it? If you do let others come into your situations, make sure they have had some success in the areas they are helping you with.

Too many people are comfortable being a passenger on their own journey towards reaching all that they desire. They would rather have someone else put in the hard work and effort on their behalf. They have the whole process sorted out (or so they think). It is like the flying experience, really. They would like just to sit there, be served by others with all the nice food and beverages and arrive at their destination refreshed, with the only effort needed to pick up their bags from the baggage carousel. What we all need to do is have a sense of ownership over our direction.

Let me give you an analogy. Many of you reading this book may have at some point hired a car, whether it was on holiday, for work, or because your own car was out of action for a while. It might be a car that was a lot nicer and newer than the one you owned at that time. As you pick up the vehicle from the car rental company and sit in the driver's seat of the near-new vehicle, a sense of excitement or thrill may go through your head. This will be a new and exciting experience for you. You can't wait to get going on your journey.

Along the way you might put the foot down a little bit harder than you normally would in your own car just so you can feel a bit more of the power, you might turn up the volume of the new stereo a bit louder than you normally would without fear of the speakers blowing up, you might even turn on the air-conditioning as this is something you don't have in your own car. You are in motor vehicle heaven, albeit only for a few hours or even a few days. You are totally engrossed in this experience.

Then comes the time when the party is over, it is time to take the car back. It is time to go back to your own vehicle. You sit in your own car and the feeling just isn't the same. But while the experience was great and you thoroughly enjoyed yourself, the reality was that the car was never yours to keep, only to enjoy for a short period of time. You don't have ownership of that car, so no matter how enjoyable the experience the unfortunate fact is that you had just that: an experience. If you would like that experience to last longer, then it will come at a higher price.

This is unfortunately how some people approach their dreams and goals—they have 'rental experiences' with them. Deep down they believe that they will have to go back to their old way of living, their old way of thinking. They experience some level of achievement that is better than their normal outcomes, which is fantastic, but they don't build upon those outcomes. While they enjoy the time they are having, they don't pursue the experience further. By not working on the longevity of those goals and its outcomes, their feelings become those of frustration, and the constant work is eventually given up on.

These people are enjoying the moment instead of working further towards making that short-lived experience a lifestyle choice that can be built on even further. After a while they slip back into the old way they were living because it is more comfortable than pushing on. Then what they do is try to put down those who have achieved their goals and dreams to justify their own failings.

What we all need to do is to create an atmosphere and environment that takes the rental mentality out of our heads and replaces it with permanent ownership. What are you actually in control of? For some, the only area that you are in total control of is your lack of direction. Are your dreams, goals and directions under your control, or are you just hanging on, trying desperately not to let go of something that is way out of control?

I don't know if you have ever been jet skiing. I loved going jet skiing when I was younger. Out in the middle of a lake or on the river, just going as fast as I could, doing as much as my skill would allow me to do. The only problem I had was, when a jet ski gets a bit out of control and you don't manage to correct it straight away, it gets more unmanageable as the seconds tick away. Soon enough you are trying to control this machine that is basically uncontrollable. The more you try and correct it the further it gets out of control. The best way for me was to fall off, that way the engine cuts out and you start again along the way.

This is how most of us end up with our lives. We seem as though we are in control until a little ripple comes along. Then by trying to correct our direction (most of the time through panic) we overcorrect, causing a flow-on effect, and sooner rather than later we are trying desperately to hang on to this thing called life; then it becomes all to hard, we start questioning our choices and just fall off. The problem is that many of us forget to get back on and start again. We just float around in our own lake of regret.

Too often we don't correct the little things as they happen. We let them slip by, hoping that nothing will eventuate from them. Then another little issue comes our way, and because there weren't really any negative results last time we let things go, we decided to do the same again this time. In this way we create a mindset that ignores the signs that things are starting to go wrong. We are then shocked when all of a sudden we are out of control in an environment that not that long ago seemed so comfortable.

An even bigger fault is that some people who do manage to start up again fail to learn from their experience. They make the same mistakes again, causing them to slip back into their now shrunken comfort zone, too scared to give anything else a try because of a fear of falling off again.

No matter what the outcome, positive or negative, you have to continually get back on the path to achieving those goals and dreams. The more you learn about why you made a mistake, and about what led to that mistake, the bigger your comfort zone will become. I am not sure about you but I want to live within a big comfort zone, and I want it growing more and more every day, not shrinking to the point that I am restricting myself from trying anything new.

Failing to reach your goals and having difficulties along the way is all part of the process. Reaching your goals isn't about what you get at the end. It is all about learning the lessons about who you are, what your weaknesses are and what you need to change along the way. To do that you need to have a sense of control about you and your situations.

If you are not happy with where you are right now, then change it. It might sound too easy but that is exactly how simple it is. Take charge; take control of your destination. Take control of the methods whereby you are going to reach those goals you have set for yourself. Stop blaming everything and everyone except yourself as the reasons you have fallen short of reaching those goals so far.

There will no doubt be areas of your life that you have under control. The easiest way to fulfilling all that you desire is to identify the principles and methods that work in those areas you are good with, and apply them to the areas you are still having problems with. As human beings, we sometimes forget to learn from life's experiences.

When I started Attitude Inc.® I had no money; I was useless at saving money. Over the last eight years the biggest lesson I have learnt wasn't how to be a great businessman, nor was it about how many new and interesting products or designs I could come up with. It was learning how to handle and control my money. I let my business and my success teach me a life lesson.

What have you been struggling with that you could control and master only if you let your life's experiences teach you?

Life has to be mastered. I am yet to meet anyone who has fully mastered his or her own life. But I have met many people who are controlling their lives, controlling their destiny purely because they have maintained the principle that they are not going to allow others to dictate to them where they will end up.

Remember, if you are controlling something, then you are in charge of its direction. Just like the pilots in those planes that I hate being in, you are the one who is directing your outcomes. You are the one steering your life in your chosen direction. As soon as you hand over that control to someone else, then they are the ones who have the ability and permission to control your destination.

So start now, take control. Be a control freak with your goals, dreams and direction. You may surprise yourself.

Take a risk | 14 |

14

The topic of this chapter may seem surprising after I've just stressed the importance of being a control freak . . . but read on.

I believe that we all fall into one of two groups when it comes to taking risks: those who take risks and those who don't. Simple really, isn't it? I know that I have probably just blown you away with my insight(!), but someone has to do it. I have always said that everything in life and in business is quite easy. It is people who tend to complicate things all the time.

Risks at times are misunderstood. Many people see taking a risk as the last resort. Because they think that it is the last resort, they then make rash decisions, thus putting their dreams and goals further at risk. This type of thinking is what I want to challenge.

I want to show you that by sometimes taking risks, we will surge ahead in our pursuit of our goals and dreams. But I also want to show you how not to lose everything when taking those risks—which is where being a control freak still comes into the picture.

The biggest mistake I believe people make when taking a risk is that they don't understand that there are two types of risk. First there is just the plain old risk (or uncontrolled risk). This is the choice or decision that you have made regardless of the consequence: the outcome is really up in the air. Anything could happen and you will just have to wear the outcome, like it or not. There is no element of control to this risk. Second, there is the 'calculated risk'. This is the kind of risk that I want to show you can be very effective in your pursuit of what you want. I want to focus on this second risk, the calculated risk, as I believe that if you really understand what I'm on about, it can open up a whole new way of thinking and operating for you.

So what is a calculated risk? 'Calculated' is just that. You need to work out what the worst possible result can be BEFORE you take that risk. You need to understand the whole process before you start. Too many people in business make decisions and take risks with the hope of growing their business without for one second giving any thought as to what they may lose if the risk doesn't work out.

I am not sure about you, but after having nothing for most of my life, there is no way I want to go back to that stage. That means that I am going to make sure that every decision is going to take me in a forward direction. Sure, I have had to take some risks during my time in business. But after taking a few with disastrous results, I realised I had to work out some way to minimise the potential damage that those risks brought with them.

Let me explain the principle of calculated risk in two ways. First, I will give you a more personal example that many of you will come across one day; second, I will give you a business example. As I have already discussed buying a house, I will use this for the first example. Imagine you are ready to either buy your first house or move into a bigger house. You have a budget, but while you are looking around you see the house of your dreams. No matter how hard you try to get it out of your head by looking at other houses, you feel that this is the one for you. The problem is that the house you have fallen in love with is way above what you really can afford. After what you believe is a lot of thought, you decide that you will buy the house anyway. The banks are more than keen to lend the money to you, so you must be able to afford it, right?

What you don't do in the whole process is look at the worst-case scenario. What I mean by that is you need to ask yourself, 'If everything went wrong, I lost my job and couldn't afford the house for a while, what would I do? How will I get by?'

You see it is these questions that need to be asked before the emotions take over and you set yourself up in a situation that may hurt you instead of release you into all that you want. It is calculating what may happen that will help you make an informed decision at the start.

Once you start asking those questions, you will force yourself back into reality. Too many times we get caught up in the excitement and we lose perspective. The moment you lose perspective is the moment you lose control over that situation. Your efforts then aren't focused on your goals and dreams; they are focused on getting yourself out of the hole you have created for yourself.

In today's climate of everyone trying to keep up with what everybody else has, we are all too easily led into situations that can cause us damage instead of joy and release. Don't try to keep up with those around you. By doing that, all you are proving is that you are a follower. Be your own person, live your own dreams. That way your life will be more enjoyable as a result of making your own choices. Why try to live up to someone else's expectations? All you do then is create an environment of playing catch-up to what everybody else has. Who says that you will be happy living their dreams anyway?

I recently had an interview with a national newspaper, during which the reporter commented that he would have thought I'd be living in a particular suburb by now, based upon my success. What a stupid way to think. Why is it that some people view success by postcode?

My success is my success. How I choose to live it is totally my decision. I don't compare myself with others who are successful and try to match what they have and neither should you. Sadly, some people put more effort into making others notice how successful they are than into working towards their original goals and dreams.

Let's now look at calculated risk-taking from a business perspective. I have a friend who owns a crane business. The other day he spoke to me about wanting to grow his business. He sat down and showed me how much he was making out of the size crane he was currently operating, then compared it to how much he would make if he had a bigger crane. You see, all he was looking at was the dollar figure, like most people I might add, which is natural in business. What he wasn't looking at was whether anyone was hiring that size crane and how much work the operators of those cranes were currently making out of each job.

When I went through the process with him, he started to see that while he could charge a higher rate per hour for the larger crane, there wasn't any more work for that size crane compared to the smaller one. In fact the hire-out ratio was a lot smaller, which would mean less money coming in the door. Also, to buy the new crane would mean high repayments, so one slump in his business would have automatically made him worse off. As he already owned his current crane outright, he currently had higher profit margins compared to what he wanted to get himself into.

My friend had been prepared to take a risk and buy the new crane. Once I worked out the figures with him and explained my theory about calculated risk, he changed his mind.

It is in the process of considering a calculated risk that we can find answers. Often we are guilty of seeing only what we want to see. We need to really assess every decision we need to make before we make it to see if we will be putting our goals and dreams at risk. You need to make sure that the decisions you make are not going to take you away from the desired result.

The beauty of taking a calculated risk is that you will know what the worst possible outcome should be. The best part of that process is, before you make that decision, asking yourself one important question: 'Am I willing to be further away from my ultimate goal and dream if this decision doesn't work out the way I have planned?'

This is a question that not many people ask themselves, yet you would think it would be right on top of the list. The minute you start asking yourself that question, the better your decisions will be. You will automatically be making decisions based on an educated thought process instead of an emotive one or a whim.

We are all guilty of thinking that we *have* to take a risk at some point, in either our personal or business lives. The problem is that we rarely calculate the losses that could occur at the end of our risk-taking process. If you start every decision by thinking of what may happen as a worst-case scenario, then you will and should be prepared for the outcome.

One of my favourite subjects to speak about is operating within our comfort zone, the processes involved in making that comfort zone bigger and the mistakes we all make that ultimately make our comfort zone smaller than when we first started—which makes it more difficult for us to step out again and try something new. We sometimes tend to operate in whatever zone is good for us on the day, just hoping that we will get the desired outcome.

The minute you take an uncontrolled risk, you are basically putting that comfort zone at risk. You are allowing your decisions, whether they are good or bad, to dictate how you will approach a future decision and future goals. If you take a risk without thinking of the outcome, then the only person you can blame for your fears and lack of advancement is you.

If you operate outside your comfort zone by taking an uncontrolled risk and it all goes bad, then effectively what you have done is reduce the size of your comfort zone. The next time you want to step out and try something new, you will have second thoughts and maybe even fail to attempt it, all due to not wanting to leave your comfort zone. You end up becoming your own worst enemy.

You see, calculated risk doesn't mean stupidity. This is important, because some people think that living on the edge, making risky decisions without properly thinking them through, is the best way to live their lives. How dumb! It is hard enough just getting close to what we want out of life without having to compete against our own stupidity and the silly results that we have made happen.

I recently had someone say to me that to grow a business you had to take risks every day and just handle the growth of that business. Dumb, dumb, dumb! If that is the way you would like to operate then go right ahead. But for me, I want to be as in control of my situations and circumstances as possible. I want to be in the driver's seat.

In taking any risk, what you are basically doing is entering into a new realm. You are venturing into an area that you haven't tried before, which means you will be a little out of your depth. Remember that fact, because what that means is that you will need to approach your new decision in a way that you haven't approached it before, otherwise you will end up with the same results as last time.

Remember one little fact: no risk = no reward. You will need to take risks; you will sometimes need to do things that are a bit way out for you to understand. You will need to step out. But you need to have a clear understanding of what it is you are putting at risk. Some people have said to me that

I never took any risks when I first started my business, as I only had $50. What they don't understand is that that was the last $50 I had to my name. My calculated risk was that I could have lost everything. We hear most often about people who risk a lot of money with their decisions but that doesn't mean that people who have no money have nothing to lose.

If with every decision you make, every risk you calculate, you think about the 'what if' factor of ending up further away from your ultimate goals and dreams, then I can guarantee that you will start making better informed decisions that will not slow down your progress.

Risks are a part of life and a part of business. Some take big risks and some take small ones. There is no rule as to how to make risks work. The only person in your life who knows and makes up the rules is you.

Remember though: your goals and dreams are your reward. With that in mind, take those risks seriously.

Ethics is not a
dirty word!

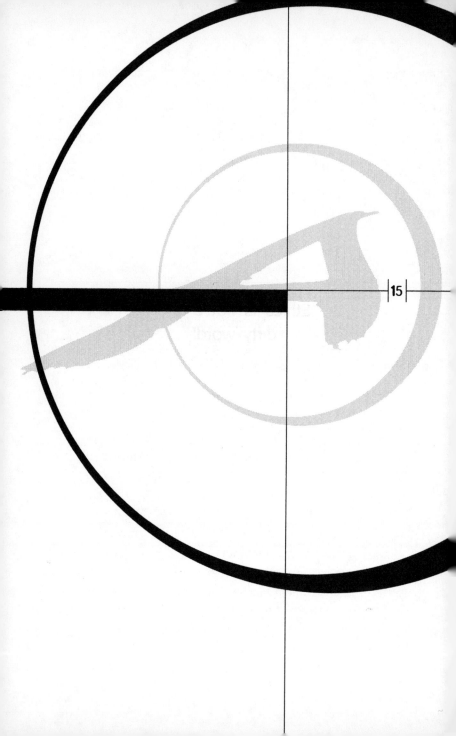

15

There are a few things in business that seem to be disappearing these days and I have to say that being ethical is one of them.

It never ceases to amaze me the levels to which some people will descend just to get ahead. Some people have no regard whatsoever for how others will fare in a deal, or for what the other party in a deal will lose as a result of it. This can even relate to your personal relationships and friendships. Too many times 'friends' of this sort will do anything to get themselves ahead without any consideration for those around them.

Your values and standards are where your ethics stem from. These values and standards need to be guarded and protected.

I grew up in an environment totally separate from what the business world can sometimes be. I was brought up to be nice to others, be kind, think of others before yourself and above all don't treat anyone other than in the way you would wish to be treated yourself. Was I in for a shock when starting my business!

While I had, and still have, those ideals, it seems that there are many others in the business world who do not. There is an undercurrent of selfishness that is as clear as day. You could sometimes be mistaken for thinking that having no ethics is a business skill. I know that I may be exaggerating, but ask anyone in business when they were last ripped off or taken for a ride. I will guarantee you will be hard pressed to find someone who hasn't had these negative things happen to them, and recently.

So what do you do? Do you change your belief system to accommodate and fit in with others, or do you stand firm to your beliefs?

I totally believe that it is in the times that your ethics are challenged that you will see who you really are and what you truly stand for. My father used to say when I was younger, 'If you don't stand for something, you will fall for anything.' This is so true, especially within the business world. We are all guilty of trying to fit in, trying to please those around us. But for what?

I probably won't have to live with my business colleagues for the rest of my life, but I will have to live with myself. That being the case, I want to make sure I don't disappoint myself. We all need to stand up for what we believe in, sometimes no matter what the cost. There are too many people out there who continually change to fit in with others' beliefs and operating structures, all the time changing and moving away from what they personally believe in. This is a recipe for failure as what you are setting yourself up for is to live through other people's experiences. That is fine if by living those experiences your outcomes are good and fulfilling, but if they aren't then you only have yourself to blame. Odds are, living other people's experiences will not have a valuable or lasting effect on your life anyway.

Each and every person who is reading this chapter right now has a destiny—but that destiny will only eventuate if you fulfil what is required. Ethics play a major role in our destiny, like it or not. If you go about living life the right and honest way, the odds are you will at some time enjoy success and it will come from a right and honest direction. If you are unethical, then sure you may enjoy a taste of success due to the fact you have scammed your way there, but it will be short-lived as that success was built upon a negative platform.

Your ethics are your own personal rules of conduct—not someone else's rules and beliefs but your own. How you operate throughout your personal and business or work life will all come down to where your ethics sit within that life.

The unfortunate thing is many of us go through our lives operating on someone else's level and playing by others' rules. Let me explain. Sometimes, when we get treated poorly or wrongly in some area of our life, we automatically react by operating on the same level as we were treated, as this seems the most obvious way to counter such treatment. But we don't learn anything at all by doing this. By operating on the same level, all we are doing is condoning and aiding the methods we despise. Sure it may feel good at the time, but there is no substance to the end result.

What we need to do is combat poor and unethical treatment with positive ethics. If someone wrongs you, don't get even by being just as nasty or bad. Respond by being better. Handling situations with a higher standard will automatically place you above the others who have wronged you. You don't need to point that out to the person who has wronged you; if you do, your reaction will have no effect. All you need to do is simply respond in a way that shows, purely through your actions, that you have put them to shame. Remember the saying 'actions speak louder than words'?

In the second year of Attitude Inc.® I was just coasting along. Things were starting to happen for me, the media had started highlighting the brand and its start-up success, and new stores were coming on board fairly quickly. I was going the best way I thought that I could at the time. To be honest, I really didn't have that much of an expectation at the start, so where I was heading was far better that I thought I would ever achieve.

As I love sports, I decided to align myself with various different sports and sportspeople as a product sponsor. What that means is I would give various sportspeople Attitude Inc.® clothes to wear for free in return for signage on either themselves or their equipment. This over the years proved to be very successful, especially in the areas of motor sports, as the company was aligned with a very publicised sport and hence was able to reach a lot of new customers at once.

One day after a few months of an association with one particular sportsperson, I received a knock on my door. After about half an hour of chitchat I was asked whether I would come into his brother's office the next day as they had a 'business proposal' to discuss. Now remember, I was green when it came to business. I was just a bloke selling a few t-shirts and having a whole heap of fun in the process. I was not educated in the world of big business. I thought that everyone was just trying to get ahead and to do so they would operate in the nicest possible manner. How wrong was I?

The next day came and off I went into the head office of this big company. I had to wait in the reception area for ages (I hate that), and then I was ushered into a big boardroom. I was asked all about my business and why I wanted involvement from this company in question. I quickly informed them that I didn't initiate this meeting and as far as I was concerned it didn't really need to happen in the first place. They then changed their approach and asked me for my wish list—if money wasn't an object, what would I be doing differently?

Seeing that I'd started my business with only $50, that was probably the most stupid question that I could have been asked at that time. Of course I had a wish list, I just hadn't particularised it because of my lack of funds up till that stage. They asked me to think about it and come back the next day.

The next day came and off I went again to their offices. Once again I was forced to wait forever in the reception area until everything was ready. I think that the waiting was more of a power thing than anything else. As I sat down I was asked for my wish list. It didn't take me very long to blurt it all out. There was nothing really special in there, just financial stuff and growing the brand.

At the end of this meeting they stood up and said that they absolutely loved what Attitude Inc.® was, what it stood for and what it could become. They saw that there was a lot of 'potential' and with their help all that potential would become a reality. They asked if I would consider a 'joint venture'. From what they explained, this basically meant I would bring what I had to the partnership and they would bring what they had (staff, services, offices, warehouses, etc.). On the outside it seemed like a very good deal to someone who was struggling to keep control of an extremely fast-growing business. They needed an answer straightaway. I was told that 'trust' is what business deals are built on so there was no need to involve any legal people—they had their own lawyer in-house who had made this deal to benefit me more than them.

I know what you are thinking: 'You idiot.' Yes I know, I was still operating under the assumption that these people did actually want the best for me. I had no reason to believe otherwise. We shook hands and I was told that I would receive the deal in writing 'very soon'.

Over the following week they told me that instead of oper-ating out of my garage, they would prefer it if I moved into their city office and put my stock in their warehouse in an industrial suburb. This seemed like a good idea, as it would take some of the extra work off my hands. They also wanted to open up a bank account at their branch in the city to keep everything under one roof.

It was at this stage that things started to go a bit funny. I opened the account under my name, but they seemed to have control over the funds. I was pulled up every time I was late into their office, yet as far as I was concerned I was my own boss. I never had to answer to anyone in the past with my business and I certainly wasn't going to start now. They started to do some in-house artwork for some of my new slogans and then I was given the invoices for them (which were ridiculously high).

I got sick and tired of travelling into the city and back every day, so I decided to set up my office at their warehouse. This didn't go down too well as they couldn't monitor what I was doing. There were even phone calls made checking up whether I was at work or not.

All this time I was still to receive anything in writing. As far as the deal was going, they were using my logo and business to promote their other products and companies but I was having to pay highly for their services. The more I raised these issues, the more I was pushed out of the circle. It didn't seem fair but there was nothing that I could do about it.

Around this time a large international company that wanted to license the Attitude name for some of its products contacted me. They had seen the stories done on me and my company on television, and knew that it was a perfect fit with their products. I told my joint venture partners only as much as I wanted them to know, as I didn't want them to take over this deal. This deal was going to be big and I was sick and tired of feeling ripped off.

Over the course of the negotiations with this new licence deal, I got to know the managing director of the new company quite well, and as a result I asked for his professional opinion about what I had been going through. After hearing everything that was happening he told me to get out as soon as I could. He could see that I was being taken advantage of, as it was a one-way deal.

The next day I packed up my stock from the warehouse and moved everything back into my own warehouse. I was threatened that day with legal action. Now don't forget that I hadn't signed any contracts so I was fairly well covered from a legal perspective. They tried to stop me closing my bank account, and even provided me with invoices for 'services supplied' in excess of $60 000 for one month's work.

I was worried. This company was huge. They had (and they told me so) the money to keep me in court for a long time and 'ruin' me. They wanted to control my company. They were even telling their clients that they were the owners of my company.

I was not prepared to take this lying down. I stuck to my guns. I was not going to let anyone ruin my dreams. I fought it legally, which in the end didn't go far before they just went away; they knew that they had done the wrong thing by me from an ethical and legal perspective.

It would have been easier during some of that to start operating on their level. I know that I could have been nasty and devious. But all that would have proved was that I was just as bad as they were. I learnt a lot about myself during that experience that I know has made me a stronger businessman and human being. I also learnt a very valuable experience about some people's ethics that I would carry with me forever. There is no excuse for lowering your standards and ethics in order to prove yourself right.

Today, I have a business that has gone from strength to strength. I have various other businesses that are doing extremely well. The company in question no longer exists.

Each of the partners involved left to 'start their own thing' with little or no success.

Why do I tell you that? It isn't to point out how great and righteous I am; it is to show you that if you operate with the right ethics throughout your personal, work and business life, then you will surely survive longer than the sharks out there that don't. If your foundation is one of bad methods and underhanded principles then that is what you will be dealt back.

Being ethical is about being moral. Sometimes you may be technically right, you may even be legally right, but are you morally right? Is just proving that you are right going to jeopardise the lives of others around you?

Remember, your ethics will be the true marker on where you will end up in life. While you may be able to cut some corners in life and in business, you will never be able to cut any ethical corners. If you do, then you have no right to complain about the outcome. Reaching your goals by being unethical will leave you with nothing but an empty sense of accomplishment. The idea is not to hurt those around us on our journey towards all that we want, it is to help them achieve what they want out of life.

Be an example. Don't lower yourself to other people's standards.

Generosity 16

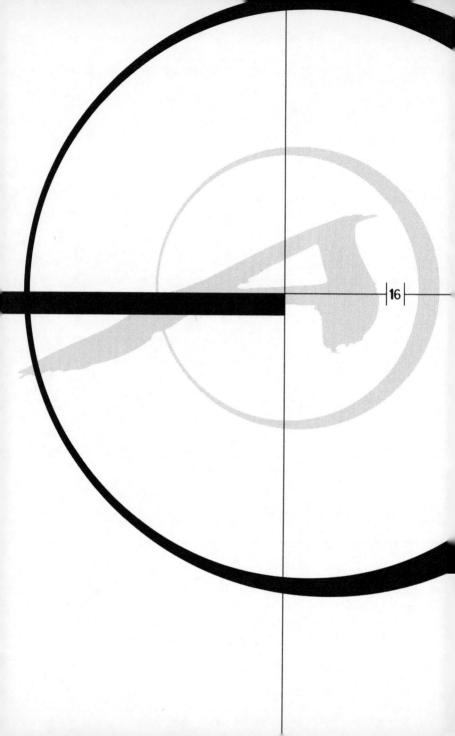

16

The subject of generosity is rarely mentioned, and when it is, I believe it is not really understood properly. Some people don't even like the word 'generosity'. They think that it only has to do with money—but that's not the case. If you want success in your life, if you want to reach the potential that we all have within us, the notion of being generous is something that you need to grasp. The principle of giving, once you understand it, will bring a whole new level of fulfilment to your personal and business life.

In today's world the emphasis is so much on ourselves that we are in danger of forgetting about helping one another. Please don't think that this chapter is intended to make you feel guilty or bad; it's just the opposite. I want to show you that sometimes, maybe even all the time, we can be better people and live our lives on a greater scale by learning lessons from those around us who use this principle. It is all too easy to pick up bad habits from our friends and colleagues, but after reading this chapter I am hoping you will see that it is just as easy to pick up on the great lessons to be learnt from those you come in contact with every day.

There is a habit these days of keeping everything to our-selves. Many of us don't want to share with others just in case they might become 'better' than we are. That is okay, that is a natural human response. But it is one that will keep you restricted in achieving your bigger picture.

Too many people these days are selfish with their time, selfish with their efforts, selfish with their advice and selfish with their money. While I was writing this chapter, I was treated to an extraordinary demonstration of selfishness. I'd gone to bed early as a result of a bad cold. Vanessa came in to tell me that someone had just rung to ask for my help, a woman who had been very rude when she wasn't able to talk to me. I decided to ring her back straight away. During our phone call she insisted we sit down that week, as I just 'had to help her'. I told her that was impossible, as I had a number of speaking engagements and in my spare time I needed to finish this book. I thought that we finished the conversation on a positive note and I went back to bed.

The next day when I opened up my email there was one from this woman. She tore shreds off me. She took me to task for everything. She pointed out that it was now my responsi-bility to help others, and as a result of me not being able to help her she was going to the media to let them know that I 'never help anyone'. Her comments really got to me that morning. The one thing I really have tried to maintain is some level of being accessible.

I picked up the phone and rang her. I have to say I wasn't

in the best of moods after reading her email. I asked her to explain why she felt she had the right to demand my time. I quickly informed her that we all have choices in life. My choice is whether I do or don't help some people and as far as I was concerned I had made the right choice the night before. She swore at me and hung up. She was never going to be pleased, because she expected everyone else to bow to her beck and call, to carry her along to whatever goals and dreams she had.

A few minutes later I received a very different phone call from someone I'd been happy to help with their business. They called to thank me for my efforts and to tell me that, as a result, their product had just been picked up overseas.

While it seems that it is human nature in today's climate to hang on to everything for yourself, the reality is that the minute you freely and willingly share your experiences, time and even money with those around you who may not have what you have, you will start to grow yourself—sometimes way beyond where you were in the first place. I am not talking about giving all your money away and living in poverty. What I am talking about is understanding the concept of putting others first, helping those who have yet to reach where you are in life.

I want to tell you about two people who came into Vanessa's and my life about six years ago. This is an example of how someone else's generosity changed my thinking and in turn my actions for the better.

I had only been operating Attitude Inc.® for about eight months when *The Small Business Show* (Channel 9) did an interview with me. Out of that interview I received many calls from retail outlets wanting to stock my brand. One of those calls was from a man named Trevor. Trevor explained that he and his life partner owned a few shops in the country, that they really liked what they saw on the television interview and would like to purchase some stock. I informed them, as I did with all my retailers, that the first order was payment upon delivery, which Trevor said wasn't an issue.

The next day I was working in my warehouse (which really was my garage at home at the time) when I heard a knock on the door. As I opened the door I nearly fell over. Here were Trevor and Kerry. Trevor, to paint you a picture, looks a bit like Sideshow Bob from *The Simpsons*, except he has a big bushy beard as well. Trevor was wearing daggy old tracksuit pants, a singlet and no shoes. The first thought that went through my head was, *Man, how is this guy going to pay for his lunch every day, let alone my stock?*

Anyway, I took them into my office and showed them the range. Kerry then went into the garage and started to pull off the shelf everything she wanted to buy. By the time she had finished, the total came to about $2500. I started to worry (about having to put the stock back when they figured out they didn't have enough money to pay for what they had chosen). Then Trevor pulled out a wad of cash and paid for it on the spot. I was blown away. I had totally judged this guy on his appearance (which is a lesson in itself, which I will discuss later). They packed their car and drove off. I did the wave goodbye thing and went back to my desk, thinking to myself that I would most likely never see them again as they were probably one-time orderers.

At this time in my life I was struggling with an illness that was wearing me out and keeping me down. It really affected me for a while and as a result I was starting to show the effects quite noticeably. Over the course of our appointment I had had the chance to talk about this just as a side issue, as well as my family and my love of cars, with Trevor and Kerry.

About two hours later I heard another knock on the door. I opened it and there was Trevor again. I figured he must have forgotten something so I invited him in. We started talking again over coffee, and he told me that he'd brought me something. He said that he was sorry to hear about my health and he just had to come back. Out of the bag he was carrying he produced a book and a model of one of my dream cars, an AC Cobra. I didn't think much of it, as I assumed he was just showing me something from his own collection, a car that we both loved.

As it came time for Trevor to leave I stopped him at his car to remind him that he'd forgotten his model and the book—but he turned back and said that he had brought them for me, to cheer me up.

I was flabbergasted. Here was a man who only hours earlier I had prejudged, being nice to someone he himself had only known for a few hours. He wasn't fussed as to who I was, how I was dressed or where I was going, all he wanted to do was put a little cheer into my life. You may think that his gesture was insignificant, but it just goes to show how something small can make a huge impact on people's lives.

That day was the start of a very long and healthy friendship. Trevor and Kerry were among my biggest stockists for years to come and have become life-long friends. At any time that I was down or sick, there they were. If I needed to get something done and I was having difficulty in finding a way to accomplish it, there they were.

As Trevor, like myself, is a big golf nut, we started to play together quite regularly. This next statement I know will embarrass him (but it will be too late by the time this book comes out) but I have yet to pay for a game of golf. Trevor won't let me or anyone else who is playing with us pay.

You see, both Trevor and Kerry totally understand and live the principle of being generous. Being generous is all about not being selfish. That may sound like a simple and logical thing to say, but how many of us, myself included, carry on in life with a sense of selfishness? All most of us do is try to keep everything for ourselves.

Reality is actually the opposite of what we are trying to accomplish. You see, by keeping everything to yourself, all you then do is close off your options to bring about release. Let me explain. The minute you give something away, whether it is finances, information or even advice, you will automatically invite good things to come back to you. I am not talking spooky stuff; I am talking about being blessed.

Being selfish is one-dimensional. The minute you become selfish with your success, you will have to control every outcome. But if you apply the principle of being generous with everyone you come in contact with, then the potential rewards you will get in return are three-dimensional. You will have people wanting to repay your generosity without you even wanting or expecting it.

Now that's the way I want to live!

I like being around people who challenge me to be better. Not by what they say, but by how they live. Being around people who are encouraging you to constantly better yourself becomes infectious. After spending any amount of time with Trevor and Kerry you are forced to change your approach to your own life.

I am not saying that these two people don't have their own issues in other areas of their lives. They may. I don't really know. But what I do know is that it is because of these two giving people that I believe I have been able to adjust to the rapid growth of my company and its success a lot easier, while staying as grounded as I can.

I know what some of you may be thinking already: 'That's fine for them, Justin, but I don't have heaps of money to give away.' That is fine. I am not suggesting that for a minute. What is it that you *do* have? What is it that you are good at that you are able to bless others with? Is it time? Is it your skills or knowledge? Only you know what the answer is.

Those of you who have read my first book will know that I was raised in a Christian home and that I am the son of a Christian minister. The principle of giving was always one that I understood and watched my mother and father live by.

One thing about my success that I love is the fact that it has opened me up to be able to help others reach their own success. I can't stand it when people become successful and then don't help others less fortunate or those who have yet to discover their own potential.

I have a saying which I love telling my audience wherever I speak: 'You are not successful unless you are making others around you successful.' You see, too many people think that success is only about getting all that you want without worrying about anyone else along the way. Some people have the small-minded and misguided theory that when they *reach* success, then they will help others.

Don't be so naive. That mentality is rooted in selfishness. So why would you think that as soon as you get to where you want to get to, you will change your mentality to one of wanting to help? There is an old saying that basically proves this same point: 'You aren't a leader unless someone is following you.' The true measure of success, as far as I can see, is how many people want to shape their personal life, business life and even friendships upon the same methods and style as you.

Just as with Trevor and Kerry, by being generous in what-ever area of your life that you are able to give, you will be blown away with what will come back to you. Call it karma, call it blessing, I really don't give a toss what you call it, but the nicer you are, the more generous you are to others, the more your life will expand.

I am not in any way suggesting that if you give your money away you will get more money back. Not at all. What I am saying is that by being generous with your time, your advice and yes, even your money, you will open up a new part of yourself that will feel better than having all the money in the world in the bank. It is that single sense of seeing what the bigger picture is (and that bigger picture isn't you) that will be the key to unlocking further success. You are expanding your mentality by taking yourself and your selfish motives out of the picture.

The one area that I would like to challenge you about at the end of this chapter is whether or not you should be selective about who you are generous to.

All of us sometimes make assumptions about people based on the way they look or even the way they act (as I did with Trevor). Sometimes I am on the receiving end of such assumptions. I am amazed to this day by the way I am sometimes treated when I walk into a car dealership. I am judged by the salespeople as to whether I can afford a car purely on what I am wearing or the way that I look. It always makes me laugh, because I want to buy a car that the salespeople can't afford for themselves—but they still judge me on appearance. As far as I am concerned, it is the salespeople who have to impress me, not the opposite.

Using this analogy, I have had to pull myself into check on numerous occasions to make sure I am not treating others who come to me for advice in the same manner. Not as to whether they can afford me (that's not what I am talking about), but whether I think they will even take my advice. I have had to let that thought pattern go out of my head, as it was ruling my decisions to help some people.

I now realise that it isn't up to me to make sure they listen; that part is up to the person who has come to me for advice. The only responsibility I have is to make sure I share my experiences and advice to the best of my ability.

You also need to be aware that there are serial leeches out there. There are some people (and you may have some around you at this point in your life) who just want to take, take, take all the time. They don't give a second thought as to what they are getting, and they don't even thank you for your generosity. But if you dare say no to them, look out.

I have one rule with people I give advice and help to. That is, if and when they reach success, they then need to help others who are wanting advice, or are needing some help.

The feelings of satisfaction I have after spending time with people who come to me for advice about their business or ideas are far greater than the feelings that come from selling 1000 t-shirts. It is the bigger picture that we need to look at. And that picture is to make an impact in EVERYTHING we do and on EVERYONE we meet.

Try it. I dare you. So, what are you waiting for?

www.justinherald.com